Measuring media audiences

Revealing for the first time in non-technical language exactly how audience measurements are taken, their complexities and their limitations, this book provides the definitive survey on measuring media audiences.

Television ratings are perhaps the most publicly visible form of audience measurement. These, along with other measures of television audiences, radio ratings, readerships of newspapers and magazines and admissions to cinemas, are used to judge the success or failure of media output and consequently to determine the expenditure of vast sums of money.

Measuring Media Audiences contains a chapter on each of the media plus a comprehensive introduction. The contributors, all experts in their fields, discuss their areas with an incisive comparative approach, drawing on examples from across Europe. The book will be of primary interest to teachers and students of marketing, media and communication studies and to managers in companies using the media for advertising.

Raymond Kent is Senior Lecturer in the Department of Marketing at the University of Stirling. He is author of *Marketing Research in Action*, also published by Routledge.

Measuring media audiences

Edited by Raymond Kent

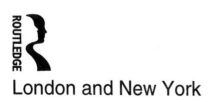

London and New York

P
96
.A83
M4
1994

First published 1994
by Routledge
11 New Fetter Lane, London EC4P 4EE

Simultaneously published in the USA and Canada
by Routledge
29 West 35th Street, New York, NY 10001

© 1994 Selection and editorial material Raymond Kent
© 1994 Individual chapters to individual authors

Typeset in Times by Michael Mepham, Frome, Somerset

Printed and bound in Great Britain by
Biddles Ltd, Guildford and King's Lynn

British Library Cataloguing in Publication Data
A catalogue record for this book is available from the British Library
    ISBN 0–415–08289–7 (hbk)
    ISBN 0–415–08290–0 (pbk)

Library of Congress Cataloging in Publication Data

Measuring media audiences / edited by Raymond Kent.
    p. cm.
    Includes index.
    ISBN 0–415–08289–7 (hbk). —   ISBN 0–415–08290–0 (pbk)
    1. Mass media—Audiences.   I. Kent, Raymond A.
    P96.A83M4   1994
    302.23—dc20   93–43868
                                                        CIP

Contents

Figures

Tables

Contributors

Derek Bloom set up his own marketing and marketing research consultancy after spending a number of years first at P&G, then the Leo Burnett advertising agency, and finally at Beecham Products, where he was Marketing Services Director. In 1982 he founded the Radio Marketing Bureau, which he ran for two years. He has worked extensively on audience research projects for the outdoor advertising business both in Britain and overseas.

Michael Brown has specialised in media research for more than 30 years. He was the first Technical Director of JICNARS and later its Technical Consultant. He has served as Head of Marketing and Director of Press Research of the Newspaper Publishers' Association and as Technical Director of the South African Advertising Research Foundation. A previous editor of *European Research*, he is presently Research Director at RSGB, a division of Taylor Nelson AGB plc.

Paul Butler is Secretary of the Cinema Advertising Association and Marketing Manager at RSA Advertising. He has extensive knowledge of the cinema advertising industry, with previous experience in the market research agency environment.

Richard Chilton has worked in the advertising, computer and cinema industries, and has been associated with the CAVIAR project from its very inception. He is Administrator for the Association of British Market Research Companies (ABMRC) and the Association of European Market Research Institutes (AMERI).

Roger Gane was Director of AGB Television International until spring 1992. In this position he was responsible for the development and implementation of television audience research services in a number of European countries. His responsibilities included the specification of meter technology to ensure the most accurate measurement of audiences, and, in association with European colleagues, the refinement of data analysis and reporting systems. In 1992 he was appointed the first Director of Radio Joint Audience Research Limited, a company set up jointly by the BBC and the Association of Independent Radio Companies to manage the new joint audience research system for radio in the UK.

Raymond Kent is Senior Lecturer in the Department of Marketing at the University of Stirling. He joined the University in 1970, originally as Lecturer in Sociology. He has published books on the history of British empirical sociology, and is author of *Continuous Consumer Market Measurement* and *Marketing Research in Action*, also published by Routledge.

Trevor Sharot is currently Research Director of the AGB Television division of Taylor Nelson AGB plc. Since joining AGB in 1975, he has helped establish new peoplemeter measurements in many other countries, and has also headed the research function for each of AGB's market measurement divisions. Prior to this he was Lecturer in Statistics and Economics at Aberdeen University. He is a Chartered Statistician for the Royal Statistical Society and has published a number of papers on weighting, estimation and panel research.

Tony Twyman operates a consultancy service in media, communications and research. He is Technical Director of BARB (Broadcasters' Audience Research Board) for television and Technical Consultant to the Independent Radio Companies. He played a leading part in setting up RAJAR (Radio Joint Audience Research). Other consultancies cover readership measurement and monitors of opinion about advertising and environmental issues. He was formerly Joint Director of RBL (now Research International) and earlier a Director of TAM, holder of the first UK television audience research contract.

Preface

The producers of television and radio programmes, the makers of films and videos, broadcasters, newspaper and magazine editors, media owners and advertisers, all require information about their audiences. Advertising agencies, media consultants and market research companies also need data on the audiences to all the media in order to be able to advise their clients or to undertake work on their behalf. The 'ratings' achieved by individual broadcasts, television channels or radio stations, the circulations and readerships obtained by the print media, cinema attendances and passages past outdoor commercial posters are all crucial to those involved in the industry, since such measures are the basis for determining the success or failure of media outputs, and constitute the 'currency' for negotiating advertising space or time; but how do we know how many people are watching, listening, reading or seeing media outputs? How do we find out what sorts of people they are? What do they think of the programmes or printed materials?

There is little literature readily available in book form to students of marketing or media studies interested in how media audience measurement actually takes place. Yet this is a particularly fascinating time to be looking into how television and radio audiences are measured, and how newspaper and magazine readerships are estimated. There are many changes currently taking place both in the technology of the media – for example, the development of satellite television – and in the way contracts for undertaking such measurements have recently been or are in the process of being renegotiated.

The idea of this book is to make widely available detailed explanations and analysis of the techniques used for estimating the size and structure of audiences to the major media. To non-specialists the world of media research is sometimes seen as esoteric and complex; a closed specialist area with its own jargon and history of development. Yet there are hints of controversy that reach the general public, for example the recent campaign in the press suggesting that audience estimates for television grossly over-state the number of people who actually watch the advertisements – and that press advertising is, of course, more cost effective.

One thing that will become abundantly clear to any reader of these pages is that audience estimates are just that – estimates – and that different estimates are produced by using different techniques. It is therefore crucial to understand these techniques to be able to interpret the various audience measures available. The contributors to this volume have all been careful to explain technical terms and to avoid jargon. They reveal – probably for the very first time – *why* measuring audiences is complex and needs to be approached with considerable caution.

The focus of this volume will be primarily on the UK, but comparisons with the rest of Europe are made by a number of contributors. Each author explains:

- the historical development of audience research in the medium in which he is an expert,
- the different systems that are used both in the UK and in the rest of Europe,
- details of the techniques used in the UK, including the organisations involved, the sampling techniques used, the fieldwork and data-capture instruments employed, the analysis and utilisation of the results, and the limitations and problems of the current procedures,
- future developments and trends.

The contributors are all top experts in their field and have worked with the media for many years. Some are directors of research in the market research organisations contracted to carry out the audience research; some are consultants to the various bodies charged with the responsibility for ensuring that research into audiences is carried out according to specification. (See the List of Contributors, p. ix, for a biographical note on each.) The end product is a book that probably will, for a number of years, remain the definitive account of media audience measurement.

The readership of this volume should include:

- undergraduate students in universities and colleges taking courses in marketing research, advertising or public relations,
- undergraduates doing courses in media studies,
- postgraduate students undertaking MBAs, MAs or MScs in Marketing or Public Relations,
- managers in companies who use various media for advertising and who

wish to understand, for example, how television ratings are derived or who want an overview of the potentials and pitfalls of measuring audiences for a range of media,

- users of media audience measurement data who wish to check out how the data were derived.

Raymond Kent
University of Stirling

Chapter 1

Measuring media audiences
An overview

Raymond Kent

THE MEDIA

The media consist of all those channels that are used to communicate with people in an impersonal manner and include:

* the broadcast media – television and radio,
* the print media – newspapers, magazines and books,
* outdoor media, including posters or billboards either on fixed sites or on public transport – buses, trams, the underground,
* cinema and video.

Some of these may be considered to be 'mass' media; others may be highly specialised, communicating only to very small interest groups. Those to whom the communication is addressed will normally be called the 'audience', although for the print media the audience may be referred to as its 'readership'. The media are primarily vehicles for the provision of information or entertainment; some television channels, some radio stations and most books are, in fact, used exclusively for this purpose. Most media, however, include advertising and sponsorship as a source of revenue. Only commercial posters are, in fact, pure advertising. Although they may provide some information or entertainment, they are not 'used' for such purposes.

THE NEED FOR AUDIENCE MEASUREMENT

Detailed information about audience size and structure, and about audience use of and attitudes towards the media and their offerings, is required by four main groups of people:

* programme and film makers, broadcast schedulers, newspaper and magazine editors,

- media owners selling to manufacturers and other organisations opportunities to communicate with an audience through advertising and sponsorship,
- buyers of such opportunities (the advertisers),
- advertising agencies, media consultants and market research agencies.

Programme makers, schedulers and editors have a potential 'market' of audiences that need to be addressed with a suitable marketing mix. Product design and specification (e.g. in programme planning and development), pricing (charge per advertising slot or price per issue), promotion (e.g. for a particular radio station), coverage (e.g. of a broadcast over a particular area) and physical distribution (e.g. of a magazine) all need to be matched against the organisation's particular capabilities and opportunities that exist in the marketplace. There will, in addition, be issues of new product development (like launching a new newspaper) and product range policy (e.g. deciding what type or types of programme to make). This process of matching is not possible unless there is at least some basic information on the size and structure of the audience for the media as a whole, for individual channels, stations, newspapers or magazines, and for particular programmes, issues or advertisements. Programme scheduling will also need detailed information on the consumer behaviour related to the media (e.g. on channel switching behaviour), and on attitudes towards and appreciation of programmes and current schedules.

Media owners operate in two very different markets: the market of audiences for their particular medium, as described above, and the market of advertisers to whom they hope to sell opportunities to communicate with purchasers or potential purchasers of the goods and services advertisers are offering. To address the latter market, media owners need to be able to convince potential advertisers that their particular medium will reach a given audience in terms of both size and composition, and that brand awareness will grow, images of the product and of the company will improve, attitudes will change, and product trial and repurchase will be enhanced as a result.

In buying opportunities to communicate with an audience, advertisers and sponsors need to decide:

- which media or combination of media to use,
- which channel, station, newspaper or magazine to use,
- how much to spend,
- what messages or content to convey,
- when, where, how and how often to convey those messages.

For the purpose of selecting which media to use and which channels, stations, newspapers and so on would be best, advertisers will require basic information on audience size and composition. This can then be related to costs to determine the most cost-effective means of communicating with customers and potential customers.

Operating on behalf of the advertisers and sponsors are the advertising agencies, the media consultants and specialists, and market research agencies, who depend on detailed information on audiences for all the media so that they can advise clients on the effectiveness of those media for achieving their objectives.

The need for audience measurement data has grown considerably in the last decade as a result of a number of factors:

- changing technology,
- deregulation,
- new sources of demand,
- increased viewing and listening opportunities,
- audience fragmentation,
- increased industry competition.

The development and widespread use of video cassette recorders and the launch of satellite television have by themselves transformed the use of television by offering enhanced control over television viewing, and a multiplication of new channels to watch. Radio has benefited from the use of car-radios, personal radio/cassette players and powerful 'ghetto-blasters'. All these developments have complicated viewing and listening patterns, fuelling a desire for more detailed and more accurate audience measurement data.

Most of the European countries have loosened state control over the broadcast media. Such deregulation has resulted in:

- the development of autonomous and private television channels and radio stations,
- the privatisation of many state-controlled broadcasters,
- increased demand for a broader range of types of programme and programme material,
- new sources of funding, e.g. from advertising, sponsorship, private capital and programme-making.

These trends have meant many more stations and channels who have the finance to spend increasing sums of money on audience research.

Not only has there been a growing demand for more, more accurate and more detailed information on audiences from the media owners, from advertisers and from advertising agencies, but also from new sources such as:

- cable television broadcasters,
- video distributors,
- sponsorship organisations,
- independent programme makers,
- financial institutions,
- the press.

Opportunities to view television and to listen to radio have increased greatly in the last decade. Besides there being more channels to watch and radio stations to choose from, the hours of broadcasting have been considerably extended with through-the-night viewing and breakfast television. The use of video cassette recorders has added considerably to these opportunities.

At the same time, audience fragmentation has meant that even the most popular programmes, newspapers and magazines have smaller audiences than they once had. The result is that market segmentation and targeting are vital. To do this, accurate and regular audience measurement data are essential.

Increased industry competition has enhanced the need for audience measurement data in a number of ways. First, competition between manufacturers and service organisations means that each must use the media effectively. Second, the growth in broadcasting opportunities has led to a corresponding growth in the availability of advertising opportunities. The media owners themselves face stiffer competition to find advertisers, which means that prospective clients need to be reassured about the size and quality of the audiences to their advertising.

KEY AUDIENCE MEASURES

Fundamental to all audience measurement are the key concepts of 'watching', 'listening', 'reading' or 'seeing'. There are two key problems to resolve:

- what behaviour counts as the activity of 'watching', 'listening', 'reading' or 'seeing',
- how long it is necessary to be pursuing that activity to be considered to have 'watched' or 'listened' to a programme or advertising spot, to have 'read' a newspaper, magazine or book, or seen a poster on an outdoor site.

For television audiences, 'watching' may mean simply presence in the room where a television is switched on, or it may entail being in the room and indicating that watching is taking place. Other systems that use diaries may define 'watching' by reference to respondents' claims to have watched a programme or an advertising spot. The development of meters that watch and recognise viewers could result in a change in definition from presence in the room to, for example, facing the television set.

A 'listener' to a radio programme may be anybody claiming in a face-to-face interview to have listened to more than half a programme (or more than half of a 15-minute time period), or it may be somebody who has indicated *any* listening in a specified period as entered in a diary. The possibilities of defining what counts as 'reading' a newspaper or 'seeing' a poster are still more confusing and endless.

These variations in definitions of media use make comparisons of audience sizes across systems difficult, if not dubious. All measures are, in the first instance, dependent on these definitions and estimates of audience sizes will vary accordingly.

The intricacies of the various measures of 'audience' for the separate media are carefully explained in the chapters that follow. However, two related concepts appear repeatedly in one guise or another: coverage and frequency. Coverage is the proportion of individuals reached by a particular medium, media vehicle or specific item of communication – a programme, a newspaper issue, an advertisement or a poster. This is, clearly, dependent on the definition of 'watching', 'listening', 'reading' or 'seeing', and on who is included in the total potential audience of interest – the universe. This may or may not, for example, include children, while 'children', in turn, may be defined according to different age ranges, e.g. 4–16 years. Coverage may appear in different guises and in some cases, particularly in the USA, it is called 'reach'. For television, where minute-by-minute measurement is the norm, coverage usually refers to the proportion of individuals seeing at least one spot in an advertising campaign, while the reach of a programme is the proportion seeing at least one minute of it. A television programme's rating is the size of its audience in the average minute expressed as a percentage of the relevant population. For the print media, coverage is usually expressed as 'average issue readership', while for posters it is the proportion of a target group who have the opportunity to see a poster during a campaign.

Where the major interest is in advertising, then it is important to know not just how many people have 'watched' or 'listened to' or 'read' the advertisement, but how often. Frequency may refer either to the number of advertisements seen by an individual, or to the average frequency over the population. Coverage multiplied by frequency gives the number of opportunities to see an ad. Together, these measures provide the basic 'currency' in which the media industry evaluates its successes and its failures, and on the basis of which buyers and sellers of opportunities for marketing communications via the media negotiate.

DATA-CAPTURE INSTRUMENTS

Information, whether for the measurement of media audiences or for other purposes, is a product of the analysis of data. Data, in turn, are the result of systematic record-keeping. The instruments that we utilise for this purpose are designed to capture data in a systematic manner. The resulting data may be qualitative, consisting of words, phrases, commentary, narrative or text, or they may be quantitative, arising as numbers that emerge from a process of measurement. Whether qualitative or quantitative, data on media audiences are normally captured using one or more of three main instruments:

- questionnaires,
- diaries,
- electronic recording devices.

Questionnaires

A questionnaire is a document used as a data-capture instrument and which does two things: it lists all the questions a researcher wishes to address to each respondent, and it provides space or some mechanism for recording the responses. Questionnaires can take many forms, but a key dimension along which they vary is the extent to which they are structured. At one extreme, an unstructured questionnaire may be just a checklist of open-ended questions with spaces for writing in the replies in the respondent's own words, producing qualitative data. At the other extreme are fully structured questionnaires which:

- list *all* the questions to be asked,
- put them in a logical sequence,
- specify the precise wording that is to be used,
- provide pre-defined categories for recording the replies.

The idea of such questionnaires is that all the questions are standardised and asked in the same way so that responses from different individuals can be counted up and compared. In practice, questionnaires are often a mixture of structured, semi-structured and unstructured elements so that only a few of the questions give rise to qualitative data. Semi-structured questions arise where respondents are asked to write in specific pieces of information which then need to be classified and coded later back in the office after the interviews have taken place.

Questionnaires, whatever the degree of structuring, are of two main kinds:

* those that are completed by the respondent,
* those that are completed by the interviewer on behalf of the respondent.

Self-completed questionnaires are usually sent and (hopefully) returned through the post, so are often referred to as postal or mailed questionnaires. However, they may be personally delivered by an interviewer, either to be returned by post or to be collected at the next visit.

Interviewer-completed questionnaires, sometimes called 'interview schedules', are usually used in face-to-face interviews, either at the respondent's home or place of work, or in a public place such as a shopping precinct or airport lounge where potential respondents may be approached and asked if they would help with a survey by answering a few questions. However, the use of the telephone for marketing research is increasing, and questions may be addressed using that medium. As with face-to-face interviews, answers may be recorded on a questionnaire or may be entered directly into a computer.

Diaries

Diaries are distinguished by the fact that they capture data on consumer behaviour longitudinally, that is, on an individual-by-individual basis over time. Furthermore, they require the respondent to complete an entry every time that behaviour occurs over the time period to which the diary refers – often a week, but may be two weeks or longer. Diaries thus record behaviour which is normally repeated at fairly frequent intervals, and which it would be difficult for a respondent to recall all at the one time in a questionnaire. Normally, attitudes are not measured in a diary, since such a process may well influence the consumer behaviour being recorded. Thus if a respondent indicates certain negative views concerning a programme, then he or she may well be tempted to swap channels next time it is broadcast in order to appear more 'consistent'.

Normally, diaries are self-completed; they may be placed personally by the interviewer, or sent by post, and may be collected personally or returned by post. Diaries may relate to individual consumers or to household activity. In the latter case, one person (usually the housewife) is made responsible for diary completion for the whole family.

Some media diaries are fully structured or pre-coded with a listing of all the channels, stations or even programmes that may be received in an area. This, however, will normally require many versions of the diary for different parts of the country. If programmes are listed, then last-minute changes to broadcast schedules may be overlooked. Other diaries may be unstructured, leaving respondents to write in channels, stations or programmes as appropriate. While this means that one version of the diary will cover the whole country, the effort required from the respondent is considerably increased, while elaborate postcoding systems may be needed for the analysis of diary entries.

Media diaries tend to arrange entries by time segment on a daily basis, often in 15-minute or 30-minute periods down the left-hand side of the page. The channels, stations or programmes will be listed or entered across the top. The respondent is then asked to indicate all segments in which listening or watching took place. Diaries for the print media will be more like product diaries, arranged on a newspaper-by-newspaper, magazine-by-magazine basis.

An advantage of a diary is that it acts as a 'reminder' to respondents and this tends to improve completeness and accuracy of reporting. As explained in Chapter 4, diaries for radio, for example, tend to produce more 'listening' than questionnaires that ask respondents to recall what they listened to 'yesterday'.

In considering the overall layout and design of diaries it is necessary to bear in mind the potential sources of error in diary-keeping:

- The diary-keeper forgets to enter listening, viewing or reading in the diary. This will often be because instead of making entries as they go along, many respondents will try to remember after a couple of days or even at the end of the week before sending the diary off.
- The record-keeper makes an entry, but makes a mistake on the details through faulty memory or erroneous recording.
- The diary is deliberately falsified either by omission of some media use, or by the inclusion of imaginary uses.
- The diary-keeper is unaware of media use activity by other members of the household.

All of these sources of error may be affected by a number of factors, for example:

- the type of programme, newspaper or magazine,

- the frequency of media use,
- the position of a page in the diary,
- the position and prominence of the entry on the page,
- the complexity of the entry,
- the overall length and workload involved,
- the method of contact between researcher and respondent.

Electronic recording devices

The use of electronic recording devices in media research is currently limited largely to television. Their use for radio, the print media and poster audience research is limited by the complexity of the environment in which the media-use activity occurs, and by the capital expenditure involved. Chapters 2 and 3 describe the different set meters and 'people-meters' used for television, and hint at the possibility of passive sensing devices for the future.

Capturing media data

The broadcast media have used all three instruments of data capture at various points. Print, cinema and poster audience research have not, to date, been able to make a lot of use of electronic recording devices; all three have tended to rely on questionnaire surveys rather than diaries, although, as explained in Chapter 5, diaries have been used to measure readership, and for poster research, which, additionally, unlike other media, also uses observation (see Chapter 6).

The instruments of data capture for researching media audiences are normally used within systems for continuous research, which takes measurements on a regular basis in order to monitor changes that are taking place. There is typically no envisaged 'end' to the research process, which will continue until the contract with the research organisation providing the research is finished. Such research is not normally custom-designed on a client-specific basis. Because of the expense of setting up and maintaining a system for the continuous or regular collection and production of data, continuous research is typically syndicated, that is, the research process or the data or both are shared between a number of clients. Usually this means that a large market research organisation collects the data and sells them to a number of clients, or that several clients buy into a survey conducted by the market research company. For media audience research, however, there is usually a joint industry body that specifies the research and contracts a market research company to undertake the research on its behalf. These joint industry bodies are described below.

Some continuous research really is continuous in the sense that interviews are conducted every day of the year, even though aggregation of the results may take place weekly, two-weekly or four-weekly. Other research, which some purists might argue is, strictly speaking, not continuous, is conducted at regular intervals with a gap between periods of data collection. The continuity of data collection, whether periodic or not, may be achieved only in one of two ways:

- obtaining data from the same individuals, households or organisations on a continuous or regular basis,
- picking a fresh sample of respondents every day or every measurement period.

Panel research uses the first procedure and regular interval surveys the second. In marketing research a panel is a representative sample of individuals, households or organisations that have agreed to record, or permit the recording of, their activities or opinions in respect of an agreed range of products, services or media-use behaviour on a continuous or regular basis. Panels are used mostly either to provide quantified, grossed-up estimates of market characteristics (market measurement panels) or of the use of the media (media panels). For the most part they measure behaviour rather than attitudes, since there are problems in asking respondents their attitudes towards products on repeated occasions. However, for the purpose of evaluating television or radio programmes, television opinion panels or listeners' panels are asked their opinions of the programmes they have watched or heard.

Regular interval surveys are surveys of respondents carried out on a continuous or periodic basis using independent samples for each measurement period. Like panels, they are used for market measurement and for media usage, but, in addition, they are used by the Office of Population Censuses and Surveys (OPCS) and other government bodies for collecting various forms of government statistics.

AUDIENCE ESTIMATION

Whatever the particular audience measure being used, and whatever the method of data capture employed, data are invariably captured not from the whole population, but only from a sample, so all audience measures are estimates achieved by expanding the sample result up to the population from which the sample was drawn. In reporting television or radio ratings, newspaper readerships, cinema attendances or passages past a poster, it is only too easy (or too convenient) to forget the various sources of error associated with sampling techniques. These errors may be systematic (resulting in bias) or random (resulting in variance).

Systematic error arises where the sampling procedures used bring about systematic over or under-representation of certain types of people or types of household. This means that *all* samples drawn from a population are likely to produce estimates biased in the same direction. This may be a result of:

* using selection procedures that are not strictly random,
* incomplete coverage of all the individuals or all the households defined as part of the population,
* non-respondents being unrepresentative of population.

Even an unbiased selection procedure will often produce samples with profiles differing from that of the population. Several random, unbiased samples drawn independently from the same population will show a degree of variation from one sample to another. The resulting error in an estimate will depend on two factors: the size of the sample being drawn, and the variability in the population of that particular variable. Probability theory may be used to define the limits within which we may be confident with a specified probability that the actual population figure lies.

In addition to sampling variation, there are errors that are unconnected with the sampling process and might arise whether a sample or a complete census is undertaken. These include response errors, interviewer errors, recording errors, and non-response errors. Asking people about their 'normal' viewing or listening, what they actually watched or listened to yesterday, or getting them to fill in diaries are all subject to memory failure, misunderstandings about the questions, or plain dishonesty. Twyman in Chapter 4 reports the results of research into the effects of some of these factors.

Interviewers sometimes make mistakes when recording answers; sometimes they interpret or approach questions in different ways, obtaining systematically different responses from other interviewers. Push-button meter systems are subject to the error of panelists forgetting to push their buttons, or pushing the wrong buttons, or doing it for somebody else.

In any interview situation there will be people refusing to respond or who cannot be found. What is done about refusals and non-contacts depends largely on the sampling techniques used, but these will, in any event, often introduce errors and biases, especially where non-respondents are in any way systematically different from respondents.

Once established, audience measurement systems provide vital information on which advertisers and programme planners make decisions. Yet in some quarters they are distrusted – particularly when, for example, a programme suffers or dies because of poor audience ratings. Measures, it is sometimes argued, are inaccurate, or at least, as explained above, they are only estimates. The samples on which they are based are sometimes seen to be too small to give results with an acceptably low sampling variation. Some measures do suffer from high non-response. Different measures, furthermore, give different results, which does little to enhance confidence.

Where measures are not taken on a continuous basis they may be biased by unusual promotional and publicity efforts on the part of media owners to raise audience levels during the measurement period. Amongst panelists conditioning may take place over a period of time. Some users feel that quantitative measures can be misleading because they measure only very limited aspects of the viewer behaviour and experience.

Whatever their validity, measures may sometimes be misused; for example, they may unduly influence the output of programmes and advertising in a way that is not good for the quality of viewing or listening experiences, so that the result is the lowest common denominator in programmes. Creativity, quality and style all tend to suffer.

Although many advertisers, media owners and media planners are aware of the limitations of audience measures, in practice such limitations are rarely considered. The pressure to do daily business using some yardstick means that all deal with the same numbers. It is, furthermore, often argued that, provided errors are relatively constant, the figures will accurately reflect change over time. The fact that all measures are estimates gets conveniently overlooked and they are instead perceived and treated as the 'truth'.

Where consumer panels or regular interval surveys are used to make estimates of the sales of manufactured products, it is possible to aggregate these estimates over the year to see whether or to what extent they match with the actual annual sales that eventually took place. If not, adjustments to the estimates can be made if the error is fairly constant. For measures of media audiences such ultimate checks on the validity of the figures are not possible. Instead, they are, on a regular or occasional basis, checked against 'coincidental' measures. Viewing or listening is recorded at the moment it takes place. Respondents (who may be a randomly selected person in the household, not just the person who happened to open the door or answer the telephone) are asked, for example, whether the radio or television was switched on at the moment of the call, and if so, to what station or channel, and which individuals are present. The measurement relates to the moment of the call, so one interview or one telephone call yields a measurement for just a short period of transmission time. This makes it expensive and inappropriate as a regular method of data collection. As a method of validation, it will normally be used on an independent sample to cover a particular time period, but one that is matched with respondents using the technique being tested. The results will then be compared with the original technique. Coincidental checks may, however, be made with respondents on the existing technique, usually to check that they have performed some specific task like pushing a button on an electronic handset to indicate that they are present in the room where a television is switched on.

There are, however, problems with coincidental audience measurement:

- there may be limitations on the time of day when it is possible to telephone or gain access to potential respondents,
- telephone coverage may not be complete, especially for some social groups,
- where respondents do not answer at the time of the call, they may be called back the following day to check that they were out, or viewing but not answering the door (or telephone),
- controlling the exact time of the call may be difficult, but crucial if, for example, it is used in connection with commercials,
- coincidental checks cannot measure out-of-home listening or viewing since such respondents cannot be contacted at the time, although they may be contacted again later.

A variation of coincidental audience measurement is the 'near-coincidental', where respondents are called, but questioned about their viewing or listening over the last few minutes or over the last hour. This can be useful for checking which commercials or commercial breaks they have watched or listened to.

Sample design

In audience research, sampling may be used for:

- 'establishment' surveys to determine in an area radio or television

reception, and the demographic characteristics of the survey population,
- audience measurements on a continuous or periodic basis,
- *ad hoc* validation studies or for experimental research.

Where face-to-face contact is required between interviewer and respondent it is, for reasons of cost, customary to group or cluster interviews in a limited geographical area. Sampling will commonly be a multi-stage process in which at the penultimate stage a given number of clusters or 'sampling points' are selected (sometimes in sub-stages) and allocated to interviewers. Usually, different sampling points are allocated for each measurement period. The selection of the sampling points themselves is normally done on a randomised, probability basis, often following stratification, for example by region, rurality or voting patterns, and with probability proportionate to the number of individuals, adults, households, or whatever constitute the final stage units. Typical sampling points in the UK will be census enumeration districts, various postcode areas, administrative areas, or polling districts or wards.

Within the sampling points selected, the next stage involves selecting which particular individuals or households are to be asked to participate or respond. 'Random' sampling in practice means that the interviewer is given lists of addresses at which to call, and which have been picked out using some randomised procedure that is independent of human judgement. The interviewer will normally be asked to make a stated number of callbacks to the address if nobody is at home when first contacted, and will not be allowed to take substitutes.

The main advantage of random sampling is its accuracy. In particular, random samples:

- minimise bias in the selection procedure,
- will, within a measurable degree of accuracy, reproduce *all* the characteristics of the population from which the sample was taken,
- will, unlike many quota samples, reflect differences in demographic composition from area to area, and also changes in that composition that are taking place over a period of time,
- allow calculations to be made of the probability of error that are more meaningful than for those commonly (and not entirely legitimately) made for quota samples.

There are, however, drawbacks. Random samples:

- are expensive compared with non-random methods,
- are slower and more complicated,

- require a sampling frame from which to make the final selection,
- may achieve a sample that is smaller than the sample drawn, largely through refusals and non-contacts.

Quota sampling means that, within the sampling point, interviewers are given an assignment to obtain a fixed number of individuals with quotas typically on the numbers of males and females, and the number of people in defined age groups, social classes and employment statuses. Interviewers are allowed to make their own selections, and how they fill their quotas is up to them. This, clearly, opens up possibilities for bias in the selection procedure.

Quota sampling is generally quicker, cheaper and easier than random sampling since no callbacks are required and its administration is simple. Furthermore, provided quotas are filled, the overall sample composition and size will be the one planned. The main drawback is that substitution for refusals is being allowed, while, because records of the outcomes of every call or approach in the street are seldom kept, the response rate is usually unknown. In addition, quotas impose a fixed structure on the sample and so may not take account of differences between localities or changes over time. Thus, unless quotas are set by area, higher-social-class individuals or households may be over-represented in lower-class areas and under-represented in higher-class ones.

In practice, random and quota procedures often get mixed as researchers try to minimise costs and maximise accuracy. Thus interviewers may be asked to fill quotas from randomly selected lists (perhaps without making callbacks – so substitution is being allowed), or interviewers' methods of selection in filling quotas may be prescribed, for example being instructed to take every n^{th} house in pre-selected streets. 'Random location' sampling generally means that interviewers are restricted to randomly-chosen streets or locations within the sampling point and given a method by which respondents are to be selected. The quotas imposed will be minimal, for example, only on sex and very broad age groups. The result is that the sample selected by the interviewer is likely to reflect the characteristics of that particular sampling point rather than quota controls. 'Random route' means that interviewers are given a random starting point in the area and further instructions about how to proceed from one house to another and from one street to another. Random location and random route sampling are usually seen as a better approximation of random sampling than straight quotas, but without the extra costs involved.

QUALITATIVE MEASURES

Apart from the various misgivings about the accuracy of quantitative data mentioned earlier, a key problem with such data is that they tell us nothing about the *quality* of the watching, listening or reading taking place. In particular, the degree of attention may vary enormously. For television watching, only presence in the room may be recorded – particular individuals may be paying little or no attention to the programmes. For radio, 'listening' is often only a secondary activity. The radio may be used just as background, and may have been tuned in by somebody else. This makes it very difficult to determine what counts as 'listening'.

Quantitative ratings, furthermore, give no clue as to what viewers, listeners, or readers *think* of a programme, a commercial or a newpaper article. The qualitative evaluation of media outputs by their audiences or 'audience appreciation' as it is usually called, is inherently difficult to measure, as are motivations, images or perceptions. Audience appreciation is often undertaken in a separate survey using standard attitude-measurement techniques. Looking at images or perceptions of media outputs may require qualitative research such as focus group discussions or depth interviews.

Qualitative research is frequently seen as a 'supplement' to quantitative measures that will tell the programme planner, editor or the advertiser 'something more' about audience lifestyles, psychographics, programme evaluation, attitudes, images and motivations. More recently, however, qualitative research has tended to take on a more independent role, for example for determining the best context – type of programme – in which advertisements for any given product should be placed.

JOINT INDUSTRY STRUCTURES

Research into media audiences is expensive, particularly since it needs to be conducted continuously. The results, furthermore, will be of little value unless the research is undertaken to standards that will satisfy all users of the data. Many organisations would not be able to afford such research on their own; even if they could, there would be a lot of duplication and many arguments about the relative validity and accuracy of competing systems. Accordingly, in the UK (and in many other countries), each medium has set up, at some stage, joint industry committees or other bodies that are responsible for commissioning and overseeing the specification of research for the medium as a whole.

The main advantages of joint industry research are that it provides a generally acceptable currency for the buying and selling of space and time, it uses funds in the most economical way and avoids arguments about the merits and drawbacks of competing measures. There has, however, been some recent critical comment (e.g. Cox, 1988) suggesting that changes may be difficult to push through, and the fact that part-time committee members are often not themselves research specialists may leave too much influence in the hands of the research suppliers.

The original Joint Industry Committee for Television Audience Research (JICTAR) was, for a variety of reasons, replaced in 1981 by the Broadcasters' Audience Research Board (BARB), which, since then, has been responsible for commissioning television research. New joint industry committees, however, have been set up, the most recent being the Joint Industry Committee for Regional Press Research (JICREG), which began its operations in 1989 (see Holland and Shepherd-Smith, 1989). For many years radio research was controlled by the Joint Industry Committee for Radio Audience Research (JICRAR), but in 1992 this was replaced by Radio Joint Audience Research (RAJAR). For the print media there was, until 1992, the Joint Industry Committee for the National Readership Survey (JICNARS), when it was replaced by National Readership Surveys Limited, which is not a Joint Industrial Council. For the outdoor media there is the Joint Industry Committee for Poster Audience Research (JICPAR).

THE CONTRIBUTIONS

In the first contribution (Chapter 2) Roger Gane sets the scene with a fascinating review and comparison of television audience measurement systems across Europe. He argues that the development of television in Europe has, without exception, been regulated by governments which, in most cases, imposed a 'public service' remit on the original channels. In such circumstances precise audience measurement systems were unnecessary. It was not until the development of truly commercial television that was competing for audiences and for advertisers that detailed information on audiences was required. This development, however, was piecemeal. In consequence, as late as the mid-1980s, television audience measurement systems in Europe were a hotchpotch of conventional diary, recall and incompatible meter systems. Only with the growth in use of the 'peoplemeter' have there been moves towards a more standardised approach.

Gane argues that only the peoplemeter could cope with the changing viewing environment and the rapid development of new technologies, for example video cassette recorders, satellite and cable television. He then outlines the components of peoplemeter systems in general, and shows how these components vary from country to country. He concludes by looking at likely future developments towards the harmonisation of measurement systems as pan-European advertising grows, and at the possibilities for new television metering techniques that automatically watch the watchers.

In Chapter 3 Trevor Sharot details exactly how the measurement of television audiences takes place in the UK. He begins by describing the origins and expansion of television broadcasting itself, and then the development of the public use of television, both in terms of equipment ownership and patterns of viewing. He explains that the demand for television audience ratings, and a number of related audience measures, comes from the broadcasters and from advertisers, advertising agencies and media specialists. The audience measurement industry in the UK has undergone a number of changes, and Sharot describes how these changes illustrate many of the problems and features of measuring television audiences. He then turns to the research process, which has just undergone a thorough review with the award of new contracts for television audience measurement in 1991. Sharot discusses the problems of defining 'viewing' when there is great variation in behaviour at all levels of the viewing population, and the need to conduct 'establishment' surveys to provide information on the size and structure of television-viewing households. This information is also required to be able to design a panel sample that is representative not just of the UK population as a whole, but of each television region.

The AGB peoplemeter is a very sophisticated instrument and Sharot shows exactly how it works. He then turns to the recruitment and control of the 4,700 panel homes equipped with the peoplemeter, and whose viewing is used to make estimates for the population as a whole. Extensive efforts are made to ensure the quality of the data that are derived from the system, and Sharot evaluates the checks and pitfalls in the process, for example, how viewing by guests and outside viewing by panel members is handled. Sharot explains the latest developments in the methods of data reporting, the supplementary research that takes place to review ITV Area boundaries, and the coincidental surveys that are undertaken to check the accuracy of the survey panel's use of the peoplemeter.

Current trends include the growth in transmission hours, the development of satellite and cable systems, the new ITV franchise 'auction', developments in television technology, and the computerisation of data storage and retrieval. Future developments lie in the direction of 'passive'

metering, the expansion of audience reaction measures, the use of qualitative data, single-source data and data fusion.

Tony Twyman in Chapter 4 reports an extensive array of research that
has been carried out in various countries comparing the results of different
techniques for measuring audiences to radio. Measuring the size and
composition of radio audiences is, in many ways, more difficult than it is
for television, largely because of the very different contexts in which radio
listening typically takes place, but also because of the impracticability of
complex metering systems. Measurement of radio listening in consequence has to rely on the use of diaries, or questionnaire surveys that either
ask people to recall what they listened to 'yesterday', or attempts to
measure their typical or habitual listening behaviour. The results of the
review of research from North America, Germany and the UK suggest
that the levels of listening recorded vary systematically with the method
of data capture, the nature of the questioning used, and whether other
media are asked about at the same time. Twyman next turns to the
development and organisation of radio research in the UK, showing how
this illustrates the way in which it is part of a continuous research system.
A new system of radio audience measurement has in fact just begun in the
UK, and Twyman explains how the new system works. He concludes with
some comments on the specific requirements of radio advertising and the
measurement of its effectiveness.

Of all the areas of media audience research, readership research is
probably the most fraught with difficulties. A lot of money has been spent
on it, and it has produced a great deal of debate and discussion for over
half a century. Michael Brown in Chapter 5 explores in detail and with
considerable eloquence the problems in trying to pin down what the
activity of 'reading' encompasses. Metering has not been possible, and
even the use of coincidental surveys to check validity is not feasible. In
consequence, great reliance, for a variety of reasons, has been placed on
face-to-face interviews, although the use of the telephone and the diary is
growing. Brown next turns to the key alternatives for measuring average
issue readership: through-the-book, recent reading, first reading yesterday, and the readership diary. Added into the equation is the notion of
reading frequency, which allows for a calculation of the probability of
contact with the average issue. Measuring frequency, however, is as
complicated as measuring 'reading', and Brown takes the reader on a
guided tour of the problems and potentials.

Turning to the European scene, Brown shows how these vary by type
of organisation and by methodology before taking a detailed look at
readership measurement in the UK – its origins and development, and its

present format, following recent organisational and technical changes, for example, the introduction of computer-assisted personal interviewing. He outlines the sampling, the interviewing, the analysis of data, and the attempts to go beyond average issue readership to research reader characteristics and the nature of the reading event. He explains the ways in which data are disseminated and used. He finally turns to the promises and pitfalls of the techniques currently in use, and the possibilities for new technology, for example, in the use of electronic diaries, barcoding and a somewhat futuristic design for the electronic sensing of perused pages.

In Chapter 6 Derek Bloom explains that outdoor posters used for advertising are pure medium and consist of nothing but advertising. Since they are not embedded in information or entertainment, people's contact with them is casual and unintentional. They are therefore difficult to recall. Furthermore, they are widely scattered in over 70,000 locations in the UK alone. The 'audience' to posters in consequence has to be some function of the number and frequency with which people pass them and whether they are sufficiently well positioned for visibility as to constitute an opportunity to see. Each poster site is different, so any attempt to 'sample' passages, either pedestrian or vehicular, is fraught with difficulties. Such estimates, even if they were possible, would still give no clue as to frequency. The solution is to model cover and frequency statistically taking into account key input variables such as reported travel habits, the size of the town, and site characteristics. Bloom explains the various models that have been developed both in the UK and in a range of other countries. He concludes by exploring the possibilities for a computer-based geographic information system that combines textual and numerical data with digital maps.

With the revival of the cinema medium the measurement of cinema audiences has acquired fresh importance. In the last contribution, Richard Chilton and Paul Butler review the measurements taken of cinema admissions, audience composition, audience by film, audience appreciation, film tracking and cinema catchment areas. The authors explain that cinema is not directly comparable with other media – an audience is captured for a period of time and there is a sense of occasion rather than habitual viewing. In consequence, the impact of advertising is unparalleled.

REFERENCES

Cox, T. (1988) 'Media Research: Do JICs Help or Hinder?' ADMAP, July/August, pp. 50–2.
Holland, R. and Shepherd-Smith, N. (1989) 'The JICREG Project: A

Schedule-Planning Breakthrough for the Regional Press', ADMAP, July/August, pp. 15–17.

Chapter 2

Television audience measurement systems in Europe
A review and comparison

Roger Gane

ORIGINS

Television audience measurement, in common with audience research conducted for the other mass media, is concerned with establishing the level and nature of the audience principally for two types of use:

- programme monitoring and scheduling,
- advertising planning and trading.

These two distinct areas of interest are very important to understanding how measurement systems have developed in Europe. For the purposes of this chapter 'Europe' is defined as the whole continent *excluding* the former communist states of Eastern Europe and the successor republics to the USSR.

The development of television in Europe over the past 40 years has, without exception, been regulated by governments, which in most cases, at the outset, laid upon the original channels some kind of 'public service' remit. In the early days, with no competition from commercial channels, these public-service channels were not overly concerned with the absolute levels of viewing achieved, but in many cases they did have to deal with political and community pressures. This meant that great precision in the audience measurement systems was unnecessary, but on the other hand it was important to establish that the service was used by the total population, including ethnic and other minorities. Moreover, apart from viewing levels, there was frequently interest in viewer *opinions* as an aid to producers and schedulers.

Although some public service broadcasters have carried advertising for a considerable period, in most cases either the amount was severely limited or the rates at which it was sold were artificially low. As a result commercial airtime on these channels tended to be 'sold out'. This being the case the audience measurement information was not particularly important to their advertising departments. Nor was it of much use to advertisers or agencies since, by and large, airtime was available on a 'take-it-or-leave-it' basis. In these conditions, the driving force behind audience measurement systems was programme monitoring, rather than reporting the audience to a commercial or a commercial 'break'.

The introduction of commercial channels – those supported exclusively or predominantly by advertising sales – has occurred in a very piecemeal way across Europe, with the UK being the first in the field in the 1950s and other large European countries not following suit until the 1980s. As these truly commercial channels appeared, so the television airtime market developed a rough equivalence of supply and demand. In this situation, a requirement emerged for more *detailed* and more *precise* information on the audiences achieved.

The technical characteristics of the television medium lend themselves to the use of meters, and this facility could, potentially, supply both the detail and the precision demanded in the new commercial environments as they developed. In the UK, which was the first country to use meters (from 1956), this need was strengthened by the spot-by-spot method of commercial airtime buying and selling.

Although, as noted above, true commercial television in the other large countries arrived much later, in several cases the measurement system graduated from conventional methods (principally self-completion diaries) to metering well in advance of the demand of the advertising industry for detailed audience information. This is true in France (introduced 1979, true commercial television only in 1985) Germany (introduced 1975, commercial television still not nation-wide) and Netherlands (introduced 1968, commercial television only from 1990).

The meter systems in these countries were introduced at the behest of government or of quasi-governmental organisations interested in the increasing importance of television as a mass communication medium and the social and political implications of this. These meter systems tended to be closely controlled by the sponsoring organisation. Hence in France, for instance, the meter system was controlled by the Centre d'Etudes d'Opinion (CEO), which was a department within the office of the Prime Minister. Only limited technical and audience information was released to the wider industry; as noted earlier, given the limited airtime availability, the value of ratings information was in any case rather restricted.

As late as the early to mid-1980s, television audience measurement services in Europe were a hotchpotch of incompatible meter systems, and conventional diary and recall operations. Not only were the data collection methods (and accuracy) extremely variable, but the format and structure of the results were also incompatible, making comparisons on a country-by-country basis extremely difficult at best – even assuming that access to the results could be obtained at all.

However, the picture began to change quite rapidly from the mid-1980s onwards, and the remainder of this chapter will describe the developments, consider the extent to which a standard approach has arisen, indicate the limitations of the standardisation and draw attention to likely further developments in television audience measurement in Europe.

TOWARDS A STANDARD APPROACH: THE PEOPLEMETER

Apart from the lack of a strong commercial requirement for detailed television audience information in many countries until quite recently, the use of relatively simple measurement methods was also supportable in terms of the straightforward viewing 'environment' which existed in most countries until well into the 1980s. The few channels available (in most cases) were, in most households, watched on a single set, making the task of recall or diary completion relatively simple. Where meters were in use, these in the main were 'set meters': the status of the set (on/off) and the channel selected were monitored, but the viewing of individuals was determined separately, through a self-completion diary (which did not, of course, have to collect information on channel).

During the 1980s, this simple environment changed rapidly and the extent of the changes is shown in Tables 2.1 and 2.2. Although the number of channels in many countries seems quite low, these are averages and hence in a proportion of households the channel availability may be very high indeed. Moreover, the acquisition of second and subsequent television sets itself greatly complicates any manual measurement system – requiring a diary per set, or more likely a diary per household member per set.

At the same time the early meter systems themselves were also under pressure from a methodological viewpoint. Most had been designed for a single television set environment, and the growth of second-set ownership, whilst it did not prevent the installation of a second set meter, nevertheless complicated the overall panel administration and data collection and processing system.

A number of organisations commenced research and development work on more modern approaches to television audience metering. To a greater or lesser extent those developments attempted to take into account the technological changes which were transforming the television medium:

Table 2.1   Average number of channels available, 1989–90

Italy	25	Ireland	6
Belgium*	22	France	5
Netherlands	12	UK	5
Greece**	11	Turkey**	5
West Germany	8	Spain	4
Denmark	6	Portugal**	3

Notes: *Flanders only
    **Capital/main city only
Source: AGB/various sources

Table 2.2   Possession of television sets and related equipment,
          1989–90

	More than 1 TV (%)	VCR (%)	Cable (%)	DTH* satellite (%)
Belgium**	10	29	91	2
Denmark	29	38	25	1
France	22	31	2	neg.
Germany (West)	19	36	22	neg.
Greece***	20	38	neg.	neg.
Ireland	16	36	38	neg.
Italy	40	19	neg.	neg.
Netherlands	23	47	80	1
Portugal***	20	31	neg.	2
Spain	25	50	4	2
Turkey***	N/A	11	neg.	5
UK	45	59	2	6

Notes: * Direct to home
     ** Flanders only
     *** Capital/main city only
Source: AGB/various sources

- mobile or portable televisions,
- multiple televisions,
- VCRs,
- non-terrestrial channels (cable and satellite).

In addition there was recognition of both the technical desirability and the
marketing opportunities afforded by:

- rapid data collection (and therefore rapid results availability),
- an improved measurement of the viewing of individuals.

It can be seen, therefore, that there was scope for a number of complementary technological developments in the data-capture technology, which together would lead to the emergence of a much improved means of establishing the level and nature of television audiences. These new methods have become known as 'peoplemeters' in recognition of one particular aspect of their capability, although their scope is much wider than this, as will be described below.

There were two main pioneering companies in the development of peoplemeters: AGB Research, a UK market research company which had developed significant European interests by the early 1980s, and Telecontrol, a Swiss technology company with links to the Swiss Broadcasting Corporation (SRG).

AGB began development work on its first peoplemeter – the AGB 4800 – in 1981 and the earliest installations of the equipment occurred in the UK and Italy (1984) and in Ireland (1985). Telecontrol systems (Telecontrol II) were installed in systems which went live in Switzerland and the former West Germany in 1985.

These systems had two significant technological developments in common. First, the retrieval of data from the homes in which the equipment was installed was by telephone. Previous meters had used a variety of storage and collection methods – paper tapes, compact cassettes and purpose-built modules. All of these required either a visit to the home by a fieldworker or a household member to remove the module and so on, and mail it to the research company.

Under the new system the research company computer was loaded with the telephone number of the household and automatically dialled the household in the middle of the night to retrieve the meter data. Apart from being cost effective and enabling faster processing and reporting, this method also improved data quality by reducing the level of 'non-contacts' and also enabling the production of diagnostic information on the operation of the in-home system.

Second, the recording of the viewing behaviour of the members of the households was undertaken electronically. Each television set was fitted with a meter that included a set top comprising a station and channel selection monitor and a display screen, plus a portable remote control handset. Panel members indicated their viewing by pressing a pre-designated button (identified by number or letter) on the handset. The signal – infra red or ultra-sonic – was then received by the set top unit, logged into the meter system and the number/letter displayed on the screen. (The current AGB peoplemeter is described in more detail by Sharot in Chapter 3.)

In each of the early adopting markets there was considerable debate and testing of the peoplemeter system. Clearly the 'people' aspect of the methodology required the active involvement of the panel members; the task was relatively simple, but given that viewing had to be credited instantaneously or not at all, there was nevertheless considerable concern about the potential error in measurement particularly in the context of a long-term panel.

Television broadcasting and advertising and the research associated with it is still overwhelmingly a national medium, rather than an international or pan-European one. Hence the processes leading to the adoption of the new research methodology reflected the views and the degree of concern about the 'peoplemeter' technique which existed in each country's media and media research community. Nowhere was this concern greater than in France. A French set meter system was in place from the beginning of the 1980s, but by 1987 when Germany, Ireland, Italy, Netherlands, Switzerland and the UK all had established peoplemeter services, there was still great resistance in France. The recent deregulation of French television had, however, placed increased importance on the audience measurement system, and in 1987 CESP (Centre d'Etudes des Supports de Publicité), which co-ordinated audience research for the advertising industry, commissioned the largest ever test of peoplemeter services in Europe. Four research organisations were each invited to set up and run a 50–home panel in the Paris area. All four – AGB, AC Nielsen, Telecontrol and Secodip – accepted. Nielsen, the US company, had run set meters in the USA for many years, and was also running a form of meter service in France as an independent venture. Secodip was at that time the research contractor for the French meter system.

All four organisations produced weekly results, including quality control summaries for several months; in addition each demonstrated its overnight data collection facility; CESP also conducted coincidental studies to check the accuracy of button pushing and also carried out follow up interviews with panel members.

The process of reporting was confused by wrangling over the interpretation, but the eventual report confirmed the high level of accuracy achievable through the peoplemeter approach. Although the debate over the accuracy of peoplemeters still goes on in France, there has, since the 1980s, been no substantial argument over their general validity elsewhere in Europe.

CURRENT PEOPLEMETER SYSTEMS

By the early 1990s fully operational peoplemeter systems were in place throughout Europe. The situation at the end of 1992 is summarised in Table 2.3. The *majority* are operated as 'joint industry' ventures. In these cases a specification or research requirement is drawn up by potential subscribers or users of the system – representatives of media owners and the advertising industry – and relevant research companies are asked to provide tenders against this specification. A contract is awarded in due course and covers a number of years – typically five. This approach is important not only in terms of ensuring a comprehensive and technically unbiased approach, but also in refining and making transparent the precise methods used.

Chapter 3 describes in some detail the technical and operational characteristics of the UK television research system. Here, the main features of peoplemeter systems in general will be highlighted. A television peoplemeter service, in the context of available market research techniques, is potentially an extremely accurate measurement system. It is, however, also relatively complex, and several factors have to be considered:

- establishing and tracking the characteristics of the television-viewing population (the universe),
- representing the population in the peoplemeter panel through panel design and control,
- deciding who are the viewers and what counts as 'viewing',
- recording the use of television sets and use of peripheral equipment,
- capturing individual viewing behaviour,
- taking raw data through editing, weighting and processing stages so that they are ready for use,
- reporting and allowing access to the results.

In assessing the extent of similarities between the various systems, we have to contend with the fact that some aspects of the system are more tangible, or more 'transparent', than others. Partly for this reason, much of the claim and counter claim activity in tenders for such services in the early days of peoplemeter systems focused particularly on the meters themselves. Other aspects, for instance editing and processing procedures and capabilities, were much less open and indeed in cases where the system was fairly tightly controlled by a media owner group, the information was sometimes deliberately subject to restricted circulation. The trend towards deregulation of television and the published information on advertising in most markets has led to a considerable opening up of the systems.

Establishment surveys

Establishing and tracking the characteristics of the television-viewing population is undertaken using establishment surveys. Until recently, establishment survey arrangements were somewhat haphazard in a number of the peoplemeter systems, but with the increasing complexity of the market and growing concern over accuracy, formal and substantial surveys are now the norm everywhere. In all but one or two markets, these take place at least annually permitting panels to be rebalanced and population projections modified at least once a year. In several countries there has been a move to continuous survey work, typically with quarterly updating of results. This currently happens in the UK, France, Denmark, Finland and Switzerland. This is important where acquisition of reception equipment is growing at a rapid rate – as in the case of the spread of satellite and cable in respect of UK and Denmark for instance.

In the main, establishment surveys are conducted by personal interview; it is vital that the surveys are carried out to a high standard both in terms of the detail and accuracy of the information collected on the household and its television reception, and in terms of the response rate and hence the validity of the population projections. In Denmark and elsewhere in the Nordic region, some use of telephone interviewing is made because of the high costs of personal interviewing and the large distances involved in some countries.

Panel design and control

The design and control of the panels used to represent the population varies considerably between countries. The factors affecting the size of panel used are largely pragmatic and economic, although in some cases other factors also come into play. Some examples are:

- The UK panel, described in the next chapter, is the largest in Europe with approaching 4,700 reporting homes. This size is substantially the result of the regional nature of the main commercial television service and the need to have adequate panels in each region.
- Switzerland – a relatively small country in population – has a total panel of 1,200 homes, but this reflects the need to report on the three

language regions, in which separate public service television channels operate.

- Belgium – as shown in Table 2.3 – has two completely separate services for Flanders and Wallonia. In this respect, as in some others, Belgium is two countries. There is a panel of 600 homes in each.

For other, less complicated, small countries, the panel size tends to be between 400 and 600 homes – Austria, Denmark, Finland, Greece, Ireland, Norway, Portugal and Sweden all fit into this category.

The yield in terms of individuals is of course variable; 500 homes in Denmark include only 1,200 eligible individuals whereas the 400 home

Table 2.3 European peoplemeter systems

Country	Research company(ies)	Meter	Operational launch date
Austria	Fessel Gfk/Ifes	Telecontrol VI	1990
Belgium(N)	AGB Aspemar	AGB 4900	1989
Belgium(S)	Sobemap	Telecontrol VI	1988
Denmark	Gallup	AGB 4900	1992
Finland	Finnpanel	Finnmeter	1987
France	Audimedia/ Secodip	Telecontrol V Audimat A2	1989
Germany	Gfk	Telecontrol III	1985
Greece	AGB Hellas	AGB 4900	1988
Ireland	Irish TAM	AGB 4900	1989
Italy	AGB Italia	AGB 4900	1986
Netherlands	AGB Intomart	AGB 4900	1987
Norway	MMI	Telecontrol VI	1992
Portugal 1	AGB Portugal	AGB 4800	1990
2	Ecotel	Telecontrol VI	1992
Spain 1	Ecotel	Televimit 100	1987
2	Dympanel	AGB 4900	1991
Sweden	Nielsen	Nielsen Eurometer	1992
Switzerland	IHA	Telecontrol II/VI	1985
Turkey	AGB Anadolou	AGB 4800	1989
UK	AGB/RSMB	AGB 4900	1985

Notes: Portugal and Spain had two operating services in 1992, but the Spanish services were in the process of being merged.
The use of '/' under the research company heading denotes that the overall operation is split. In France the two companies use different meters.

Irish panel contains about 1,400 panel members. France, Italy and Spain all have national panels of around 2,000 homes whilst the German panel is somewhat larger and has recently been supplemented by an additional separate panel in the Lände which formerly comprised East Germany. First and foremost the design of the panel in each country must reflect the national broadcasting and reception characteristics. Again, here are some examples:

- Spain – apart from national public and private broadcasters – has television services provided by regional government stations (*autonomicas*), and these must be properly represented. For instance, the stations serving Catalonia command a significant audience share in their region.
- Ireland, although a small market, is relatively complex in that it subdivides into the area receiving only domestic television channels, another additionally receiving UK 'overspill' broadcasts and yet a third in which satellite channels are received through cable systems, mainly in Dublin, Cork and other large towns.
- Scandinavia has high cable reception and it is growing, so advertisers need to be able to analyse results for this sector of the population where additional commercial channels operate.

Before commenting on the methods by which panels are controlled, gross and net panels, and panel turnover need to be considered.

The distinction beween gross and net panels is much more clearly established in the UK than in almost any other market. The gross panel is the total panel recruited according to panel targets and equipped with peoplemeters. The net panel is that proportion of it which on any reporting day produces usable results – in the USA this is referred to, perhaps rather more clearly, as the 'in tab' panel. Until recently, many other panels did not commit to and achieve specific net panel sizes; with their greater use in commercial trading has come an increased 'transparency', and services such as that in Germany are now committing to a net panel size.

In terms of panel turnover, there is considerable debate over the relative merits of *natural* and *forced* panel turnover. The former requires that only homes 'resigning' or those 'ejected' because of unsatisfactory behaviour are replaced – in addition to those households physically moving. These factors together may lead to a turnover of 20–5 per cent each year. Forced turnover requires that the panel is systematically rotated during a period of, say, five years. It is more difficult to administer, more expensive and reduces the available analysis base for long-term analyses (e.g. cumulative analysis of campaign reach and frequency). Most European systems therefore use natural turnover.

The precise controls used to set up and monitor the balance of the peoplemeter panel vary greatly from country to country. Increasingly, however, there is a tendency towards the use of household size and number of television sets as key controls, in replacement for less effective criteria such as socio-economic status, or size of town/community. There is less acceptance of estimated 'weight of viewing' levels (from establishment surveys) which where used may guard against the long-term panel becoming one of 'heavy' television viewers.

Panel control is one of the areas which is gradually becoming more transparent, and we may see moves towards greater uniformity across Europe's peoplemeter services.

Definitions

One of the biggest potential sources of difference between the services offered in various countries reflects local opinion or prejudice rather than technology. Differences exist in terms of the:

• definition of eligible universe,
• definition of viewing itself,
• treatment of holidays.

Universe definitions initially vary to a minor extent in terms of the minimum age at which children are included in the measurement and equally at the definition of the minimum age for adults. The minimum age of inclusion is 3 years (France, Germany, Austria, Finland) and the maximum is 6 (Switzerland and the Benelux countries). The minimum age for adults varies between 14 and 16 years.

More importantly, some services exclude certain parts of the population. Most exclude those living in institutions, but the German systems also exclude 'non-nationals' from the study; however, the specification for the next contract in Germany allows for a separate panel of non-Germans.

The definition of viewing – when the panel member should press the button – also varies and the situation is summarised in Table 2.4. Conceptually, the three definitions are hierarchical in terms of their intended relationship to actual viewing activity. The lowest level of eligibility – 'present in the room' – does not impose any restriction on the respondent. Being in the same room as an operating set is sufficient. Even this definition, however, has its problems: some rooms are open-plan or

otherwise imprecise, and some 'viewing' may be done from doorways!
'Able to watch', whilst not clearly defined, means that the respondent is
physically able to watch by virtue of location relative to the televison set.
Some self-assessment of this is involved. At the highest level 'watching'
means that (in the respondent's own estimation) he or she is paying
attention to actual viewing activity. At the time of writing, the rule for
Norway and Sweden was not confirmed.

Table 2.4   Definition of viewing across Europe

Definition	Where used
In room	Belgium (Flanders), Denmark, Finland, France, Ireland, Spain (Dympanel), Greece, Portugal (AGB), UK
In room and able to watch	Switzerland
In room and watching	Austria, Belgium (Wallonia), Germany, Italy, Portugal (Ecotel), Spain (Ecotel)

Some testing of the effect of these definitions has been conducted, and
it seems likely that it is minimal. Given the primary job of the research is
usually to support advertising trends, the 'in room' definition is most
appropriate – approximating 'opportunity to see'.

The treatment of holidays is a potentially important issue. Systems
in operation in several southern European countries (Portugal, Spain,
Turkey) exclude panel homes from the analysis where the members are
away or on holiday. This will, in principle, inflate the level of viewing. A
partial justification is the tendency for people in these countries to take
holidays in apartments and so on in the same country, and with television
access. However, viewing patterns are most unlikely to be the same, and
this approach is not accepted as good practice. Various countries have
considered supplementary panels/surveys to deal with holiday viewing,
but no systematic approach has been devised.

Measurement of usage of televisions and other equipment

One of the great strengths of television audience research is the potential
ability to measure correctly, precisely and automatically the status of

television sets, VCRs and satellite and cable equipment through the meter equipment. All meters have been able to determine whether a television is switched on or off and to which channel it is tuned more or less correctly in simple situations, and the more developed ones – AGB and Telecontrol in particular – have sufficient capability to deal with all 'normal' conditions. Shortcomings which still exist in some meter systems include:

- the inability to measure mains portable sets (when moved) because the meter uses special cabling,
- difficulty in dealing with new services or changed frequencies – there is no automatic recognition of changes,
- difficulty in dealing with certain types of tuner.

In general much progress has been made in this area, but ongoing advances in television technology will continue to pose problems.

Measurement of simple cable systems (tuned through the television) is not problematic – the normal television meter can cope with this. Cable systems with a separate converter are not common in Europe – although they do exist in the UK, Ireland, France and also to a limited extent in Scandinavia. These can generally be dealt with technically; a complication is the need to obtain permission from the cable system operator to open the converter. The exception is the advanced 'switch star' systems which exist, albeit only in a small way, in the UK and France. It is virtually impossible to monitor these correctly with present technology since any television service/programme selected is received in the home on the same cable channel.

Satellite service measurement can be achieved by equipment similar in kind to that used to measure terrestrial television. In practice at this time direct-to-home (DTH) satellite is only significant in the UK, where it is correctly measured.

Probably the most complex potential measurement problem relates to VCRs. In the early days of VCR growth these were almost always ignored; in so doing systems underestimated live viewing – where the VCR tuner was used to select television channels, perhaps because the VCR had remote control and the television did not.

A number of smaller systems, or those using less-developed meters, still do not deal with this issue. (The 'viewing through' the VCR issue may have become less important as more televisions with remote controls are acquired.)

The most sophisticated meter systems permit the 'fingerprinting' of recordings made so that when they are played back the meter can read the date, time and channel on a continuous basis. This permits the calculation of the additional audience to programmes and commercials as described for the UK in the next chapter. AGB systems in Netherlands, Belgium, Ireland and Denmark also have this facility, and the Gfk/Telecontrol German system can also achieve this by reading codes carried on broadcasts.

Although most systems can cope with the essentials of measurement, in terms of a valid research system, however, it is important that the meter equipment makes it possible to include within the sample all types of household television 'environments'. With the growth of multiple television homes, VCR ownership (again multiple in some households) and satellite and cable systems, meter services must:

- be easy and unobtrusive,
- be able to cope with multiple equipment situations,
- be able to cope with equipment changes,
- deal with new configurations – different ways of 'wiring up' the television/VCR/satellite equipment,
- must not obstruct the daily life of the household.

The older versions of the main meter systems, as well as some of the other systems still in use, cannot deal adequately with all the complexities and will undoubtedly be replaced or upgraded in the near future.

Measurement of individuals' viewing

The basic principle of the peoplemeter has already been referred to, and is quite simple. All types of peoplemeter work in a similar way in this respect:

- a particular button on a remote handset is allocated to each member of the household,
- when the button is pressed, a corresponding number is illuminated on the set top display – start of viewing by that individual is recorded at this point,
- a further press will extinguish the light and the meter notes that viewing has terminated.

This approach therefore measures viewing in real time; recall is thus eliminated from the measurement approach, *but claim is not*. We still rely on individuals' activity and hence peoplemeter services are only really 'meters' in respect of the 'set' measurement.

Some minor variations exist; in the Dutch and Belgian (Flemish) systems the respondent has to press a 'confirmation' button to enter viewing – in order to prevent accidental incorrect claims; the French (Secodip – Audimat) system included a facility to enter data omitted after the event. Both of these are legitimate approaches to deal with possible shortcomings in the methodology. In general, however, the view has been to make the respondent task as simple as possible and hence the 'single press, real time' mode is dominant.

There are two additions to the functions of the peoplemeter as far as individuals are concerned. The first concerns guests or visitors. There is generally an interest in measuring these since in doing so an approximate compensation is made for the viewing done by panel members outside their own home (but in other private dwellings). The methods for handling guests vary – from simple use of unallocated buttons, to use of special button sequences to input guest entry together with sex, age and status information about the individual.

The second addition is the collection of programme appreciation information to complement the audience figures. This facility is included in the services operating in Denmark, Ireland, the Netherlands and Switzerland. In order to produce analysable information there must be a way to obtain the appreciation 'scores' systematically at predefined times. There are two methods in use:

- transmission of a special code in the broadcasts which will trigger requests for panel members to vote – by instruction on the set top display,
- downloading of 'time prompts' through the meter system so that an instruction will appear at a specific time.

The first method ensures that the prompt appears at the right point in the transmission, typically at the end of a programme, but involves additional equipment and cost and the active involvement of all broadcasters. The second can be effected by the research company (providing the meter system has the capability) and is less costly; however, it is not directly programme related and will be subject to problems of late viewing or last minute schedule changes.

There has been considerable debate about the desirability of adding this facility – its opponents suspect conditioning and/or fatigue. There is no conclusive evidence, and it is possible that the interest in programme appreciation services within the meter services (as opposed to others which run quite separately) will grow as additional aids to both programming and sales people.

Data collection and processing

In all but one case, data collection is effected by telephone, and most systems use a household's normal telephone line. The modem within the meter is programmed to go 'on-line' at prespecified times during the early hours of the morning and the data collection computer automatically dials all homes to retrieve the information. Collection of data for a single day's viewing normally takes between 30 and 60 seconds. A meter is normally programmed to repeat the 'on line' mode if it is not successfully called during the first window and response rates are usually high – 95 per cent of homes or higher. In the former East Germany, the telephone system is technically poor and ownership still far from universal, therefore the research contractor, Gfk, has installed a meter which requires a visit to the home by a fieldworker with a portable computer. This system works quite well, but there are two implications:

- the need for a larger gross panel to compensate for a higher non-response,
- an inevitable delay in processing and reporting.

Another version of an off-line panel formerly operated in Ireland (using removable data modules), but for the latest contract, given the need for more rapid information, the subscribers chose to bear the cost of installing telephone lines in those homes without them.

Following data collection, data are edited to deal in particular with:

- 'uncovered' television usage occurring when a set is switched on but no viewers are registered,
- elimination of possible multiple viewing claims – panel members choosing to be viewing more than one television set within the home.

In practice the former is much more the important issue and procedures vary from service to service. The general approach normally used is, where possible, to 'impute' a small amount of viewing (i.e. to 'cover' using adjacent information on individuals' viewing) and to reject any other 'uncovered' data.

The main processing (including corrective weighting and projection to population estimates) is the most substantial part of the process, involving calculation of viewing estimates for short-term periods, for all individuals within each household for the whole of the 24 hours since the last data were collected. (This assumes daily data collection.) Most systems process data at the level of *one minute*, although some (the Telecontrol systems) can do so at 30 second intervals. The basis of calculating the audience within the minute varies by processing system (some simply take the audience at the mid part of the minute, others look for the majority activity within the minute). The practical effect of these variations is likely to be minimal.

The processing must also link the information from VCR and satellite/cable converters with the appropriate television sets to ensure that correct channel audiences are calculated. In addition, the viewing information is normally linked with two other datasets:

- master files and demographic household information,
- transmission data – for programmes and commercials so that audiences to programmes and commercial spots and breaks can be computed as well as simply for time periods.

Transmission information is sometimes provided automatically either through additional work undertaken by the research company or by automatic feed of 'post transmission logs' by broadcasters. In a few smaller markets there may be a delay in providing transmission-based information.

Information delivery

There is a clearly discernible trend in the method of delivering television audience research results. For many years printed reports predominated, but with the potential for overnight data and the increased demands for the detailed information, these have become progressively less appropriate.

In the mid-1980s, on-line results availability was offered in a number of services – one of the first was AGB Intomart in the Netherlands. Subscribers could have overnight access to precalculated results whether by dedicated line or by dialling in. This type of service is now used in other markets.

In the 1990s, there is much greater interest in access to raw (individual level) data. In large markets, major subscribers take the entire database on tape or by download for processing on large mainframe computers, but elsewhere there is now greater use of PC systems. The Danish service operated by Gallup is the first to operate entirely on PC; others use mainframes or minis for basic processing. Gallup downloads raw data daily to clients' PCs and installs reporting software allowing users to create their own tailor-made reports. There is little doubt that increasing use will be made of PC systems for manipulating and reporting the growing amounts of data generated by peoplemeter services.

FUTURE DEVELOPMENTS

In spite of a period of rapid technological and service development for European television audience research, Western Europe now displays *relative* homogeneity in the audience measurement services in operation. The likely threads of development for the remainder of this decade are considered below.

Continuing moves towards 'harmonisation'

Following on from the increased involvement of the subscribers and users of the services in the specification and design, there have been moves to standardise approaches across Europe. In the main this has been prompted by the growing interest in pan-European advertising. The importance of this cross-border advertising should not be overstated; nevertheless, even though almost all broadcasters are still nationally oriented, major advertisers and agencies are frequently working on campaigns with a European, or at least multi-country, objective. A number of initiatives have been set up to reduce the unnecessary differences and anomalies between the services. The European Broadcasting Union (EBU) and an organisation representing European public-service broadcasters (GEAR) have been prominent in this. The most proactive organisation has been the European Association of Advertising Agencies (EAAA) which has undertaken substantial work to identify, in detail, the characteristics of all research systems. Apart from removing barriers to comparability (e.g. different age groups in analyses, different definition of viewing, etc.), the EAAA is particularly campaigning for full availability of all data for all users of the service. There is little doubt that this availability will be achieved well before the end of the century. It is, however, unlikely that we will have a single European television research database in the next few years.

Meter techniques

As far as the measurement of television sets and other equipment is concerned, existing meter technology is quite adequate for the present. They may come under strain, however, as the ways in which different pieces of equipment can be linked become more varied. Whereas at present all audiences to channels are derived from establishing frequencies or other 'indirect' technical evidence, it may eventually be essential to identify *what is on the screen* in order to be sure of the service and programme being watched. Techniques for this kind of approach do exist, but are not in active development for any meter system.

Measuring individuals' viewing

As indicated earlier, individuals' viewing is *not* metered. Because of this the peoplemeter method does not of course produce perfect information. In the late 1980s there was considerable interest in the development of so-called 'passive' techniques. This 'holy grail' was pursued particularly enthusiastically in France (and also in the USA). A test using a meter developed by a new manufacturer was undertaken in France, but the results were far from encouraging.

Other major organisations, especially AGB and AC Nielsen, have undertaken quite substantial development work on techniques based on the principle of image recognition using neural networks. The development costs are very high, leading eventually to much higher operating costs in order to recover the investment. The practical difficulties of designing and installing such equipment are considerable and the benefits in terms of improved accuracy far from certain. Given that another way of improving accuracy is to increase the overall panel size – especially useful as there is increased interest in looking at the viewing patterns of demographic subgroups – it is far from certain that 'passive' systems will replace peoplemeters in the foreseeable future. Certainly the technology/cost intercept is some way off.

Measurement in new countries

To date, meter systems are largely confined to 'Western' Europe. Plans are afoot for metered services – small scale initially – in one or two of the former Eastern Bloc European countries. The first of these began in Hungary in early 1993, initially as a city panel in Budapest. The Czech Republic and possibly Poland are likely to have meter systems in place by the mid-1990s. Although this book is concerned mostly with Europe, it is worth noting that in the early 1990s, peoplemeter systems were also operational not only in Canada and the USA, in Australia, New Zealand and South Africa, but also in several countries in South America and in a number in Southeast Asia. We should not assume that all future technical and operational developments will be instigated in Europe.

CONCLUSIONS

It is unlikely that the apparent developments in the coming years will be as drastic as those of the 1980s. Nevertheless, there will be real changes and improvements, and data access and manipulation will be at the forefront of these. Television audience research systems will continue – in research terms – to be expensive and hence to attract close scrutiny from all quarters.

NOTE

* I am grateful to Dr Toby Syfret, Consultant to EAAA, who has provided me with valuable information in the preparation of this paper.

Chapter 3

Measuring television audiences in the UK

Trevor Sharot

THE EXPANSION OF TELEVISION BROADCASTING

Public television broadcasting in the UK was started by the British Broadcasting Corporation (BBC) in 1936, transmitting to a handful of homes in London from Alexandra Palace. Service was suspended during the war, but was resumed in 1946, when the television licence was introduced, at an annual fee of £2.

The BBC's charter, due to expire at the end of the year, was extended for a further five years, and the need for a government enquiry into television broadcasting was considered. Such an enquiry was set up in 1949 under Lord Beveridge. The recommendations of the Beveridge Committee paved the way for the introduction of advertiser-supported television.

In 1953 a White Paper outlined the shape of independent television, and the Television Bill was published and enacted in 1954. It brought the Independent Television Authority (ITA) into being and laid down its advertising provisions. These included such seminal steps as forbidding both the Authority and programme contractors from acting as advertising agencies, a ban on programme sponsorship and the requirement for a committee concerned with advertising standards. The Act also laid down requirements on the amount and timing of advertising, the approval of rate-cards, the exclusion of political and religious advertising and the provision of facilities for local advertisers.

Commercial broadcasting started in London in 1955. The weekday contractor was Associated-Rediffusion and the weekend contractor ABC. Regional broadcasting was progressively established throughout the UK, reaching 50 per cent of households in 1959 and, by the time the appointment of programme contractors was completed at the end of 1962, almost 75 per cent.

Both the BBC and ITV claimed the need for further channels and advertisers were keen to have a second commercial channel. Among the issues involved in any such move was the lack of room on the VHF, 405 line, waveband. In 1960 the Pilkington Committee under Sir Harry Pilkington was established to advise on the way ahead. It published its report in June 1962 and the government swiftly reacted with a White paper. The committee had taken an unfavourable view of commercial broadcasting and its recommendation that a third channel be established by the BBC was adopted. So too was the proposal to move transmission to the UHF band, making room for more channels, better picture quality (625 lines) and colour. The committee also recommended against advertising 'magazine' programmes, subliminal advertising and extension of breaks beyond the six minutes per hour average; it also expressed concern at advertising in children's programmes.

BBC 2 first broadcast from the Crystal Palace transmitter in 1964, but the need to provide UHF transmitters across the network meant a gradual growth in penetration over the following years.

The ITA, meanwhile, still had its eye on 'ITV 2' and put proposals to the Minister of Posts and Communications in December 1971, but within two months the government announced that the decision was to be postponed indefinitely. It did, however, lift all restrictions on broadcasting hours.

In July 1972 the ITA became the Independent Broadcasting Authority (due to taking on independent local radio) and it made fresh proposals for another channel, as did the ITV companies themselves through the Independent Television Companies Association (ITCA). The first acknowledgement of the need came in 1974 from the Crawford Committee's review of the regional structure of ITV under Sir Stewart Crawford. The committee recommended that a fourth television channel be set up in Wales giving priority to Welsh-language programmes, in advance of a decision for the rest of the UK.

The Crawford enquiry overlapped with a further broad enquiry into the future of broadcasting headed by Lord Annan, which reported in 1977. Annan also supported creating a fourth channel, to be run by a new body, the Open Broadcasting Authority, but Margaret Thatcher's new Conservative government of 1979 killed the idea of another government-funded authority. The IBA (now the ITC) was to be responsible, and funding was to be provided by a levy on the ITV companies, who would in turn sell advertising airtime on the new channel in their region. These arrangements were formalised in the 1980 Broadcasting Act. In the event, the Welsh fourth channel S4C (Sianel Pedwar Cymru) went on the air just twenty-four hours ahead of Channel 4 itself, on 1 November 1982.

In 1979 each ITV franchise was put out to tender, together with a new breakfast-time service to be carried on the same channel as ITV. Eight companies bid for this contract, which was awarded to TV-AM, a consortium led by Peter Jay. The launch date had been fixed for May 1983, but the BBC pre-empted with a new breakfast programme of its own and the date was brought forward to 1 February. Nevertheless, the BBC launched its service two weeks earlier and retained two-thirds of the breakfast-time audience over TV-AM's first four weeks.

Thus did audience research fuel TV-AM's internal strife, which led within three months to two changes of chairman, the appointment of Greg Dyke from London Weekend Television as Chief Executive and the departure of all of the 'Famous Five' : David Frost, Michael Parkinson, Angela Rippon, Anna Ford and Robert Kee.

The arrival of TV-AM helped to alleviate the chronic shortage of advertising time, but excess demand remained. Throughout the 1980s, each ITV company increased its hours of programming from an initial level of about 13 hours to an average of 18 hours, using both daytime and night-time programming. It is worth noting that the actual hours of viewing barely changed, though it was redistributed over the day.

The birthplace of 'non-terrestrial' transmission in the UK is a Home Office report on Direct Broadcasting by Satellite (DBS) in May 1981. This document outlined certain options for starting a service, but was (rightly) sanguine about the cost/revenue equation.

In the following year came the Hunt Committee's report on cable. Several ITV companies had long used cable to carry their signals to pockets of their areas where reception from transmitters was inhibited by the terrain, but these were in the main 'narrow-band' systems with no capacity for extra channels. Hunt noted that cable would not expand without finance from new advertiser-supported channels.

A White Paper in April 1983, *The Development of Cable Systems and Services*, announced the offer of new cable licences and the setting up of a Cable Authority to continue the process – which is indeed what has happened, with cable now supplying about 8 per cent of UK households with their signal and annual growth of about 1 per cent per annum.

Early plans for DBS changed a number of times until the award of a licence to British Satellite Broadcasting. BSB started broadcasting in March 1990, but this service, from the Marco Polo satellite, was encumbered with a new electronic transmission standard, D-MAC, expensive to develop and capable of bringing high-definition pictures only to homes purchasing not only the receiving dish and receiver but a special TV set as well.

The already dubious economics of BSB were dealt two further blows. The first was difficulties in developing the decoder for the set-top receiver, which delayed the launch by a year, and the other was the launch meantime of Sky Broadcasting on the Astra 1a satellite. Sky Television was a company which had started pan-European broadcasting in 1982 and was registered in Luxembourg; it thus circumvented all the Home Office conditions imposed on BSB. It used standard and therefore cheaper technology. It had severe funding problems of its own, but the Astra service, launched in February 1989, had captured 800,000 homes by the time BSB came on air in April 1990.

Within six months, Sky had taken over BSB to form British Sky Broadcasting (BSkyB). With the field to itself, cash flow was much improved; it took channels on a second satellite, Astra 1b (and more recently on a third), and in July 1992 it sold the Marco Polo satellite (at a substantial loss) to Norwegian Telecom. By this time, the synergistic growth of cable and dish sales was delivering six BSKyB channels (and as many other English-language channels again) to 15 per cent of UK households, with combined annual growth of 1.5 per cent of households per annum.

October 1991 saw another major industry event: the auction of the new ITV franchises, which run for ten years from January 1993. Channel 4 also became responsible for selling its own airtime from this date.

THE PUBLIC USE OF TELEVISION

Equipment ownership

Currently, about 97 per cent of households own one or more televisions. The 3 per cent who do not have a profile different from the main population and are mostly young, low-income households. Nevertheless, because television ownership is so high, the profile of owners is very similar to the population at large.

Television households currently have the following profile:

- all but a handful of these homes can receive all four terrestrial channels,
- 96 per cent own a colour TV set,
- 74 per cent own a remote-control set,
- 53 per cent own two or more sets, but for families with children the figure rises to 65 per cent while for other TV households it is 47 per cent,
- 61 per cent own one VCR while another 7 per cent have two or more,

- 14 per cent of households can currently receive two or more Astra channels, most of them having bought a 'dish' to do so; this figure continues to grow.

These figures may be compared with the situation in 1980, when only 19 per cent of television households owned more than one set, only 1 per cent of homes owned a VCR and satellite was non-existent.

Patterns of viewing

Despite the increase throughout the 1980s in number of channels, hours of broadcasting and equipment ownership, the amount of actual viewing has changed very little. Looking at the decade from 1980, average daily hours of viewing for each year ranged from 4.9 hours to 5.3 hours per home and 3.0 to 3.8 hours per individual. Naturally, there is variation throughout each year, with viewing levels in the winter being about 50 per cent higher than in the height of summer.

The introduction of Channel 4 may not have greatly influenced the total amount of viewing but it did impact on channel shares. BBC viewing, although declining to 2.3 hours per day in 1983 and 1984, returned to 2.5 hours per day in 1989 – almost the same level as 1980. Commercial television, which rose from 2.5 hours in 1980 to a peak of 2.9 hours in 1985 returned to the 1981 level of 2.6 hours, but now accounted for by ITV plus Channel 4. ITV alone saw its share eroded from the early year level of 49–50 per cent to 41 per cent by the end of the decade.

This decline is highlighted further when one analyses the change in peak-time viewing across the ten-year span. In the early years of the decade 64 per cent of homes were viewing peak time, but this steadily declined, despite a brief respite in 1985–6, to 57 per cent, the brunt of which fell on ITV and BBC1.

Certainly the introduction of Channel 4 did not increase levels of viewing at peak time, just as the increase in the number or transmission hours failed to increase total hours of viewing. In 1980 the total hours of transmission was approximately 13 hours per channel per day. By 1989 this had increased to an average of 18 hours per channel per day with an additional channel included.

The reported decline in viewing over the decade was partly due to the rapid growth of VCR ownership. Throughout the 1980s, audience estimates did not include 'timeshifted' viewing, that is, recording a programme on a VCR and subsequently playing back the tape. This omission was rectified with the introduction of the new measurement system in August 1991. The current situation is that homes with VCRs record on average around four to five hours of material each week, equivalent to about 10 per cent of all tuning. Of this, about a half is played back within seven days and, under the current BARB rules, will therefore contribute to the published audience figures. (Some of the remaining recorded material will be, for example, follow-on programmes which were recorded because the VCR was allowed to continue recording to the end of the tape.)

VCR homes watch on average about a further two hours of rented (or bought) tapes – an average of one film per week. To some extent this viewing will be at the expense of viewing to broadcast material. In addition to this VCR effect, the audience is fragmenting, and this can be highlighted by analysing and comparing top programmes between 1980 and 1989.

As can be seen from Table 3.1, the top ten positions for 1989 are all showing audiences of between 2 million and 3 million individuals lower than their counterparts in 1980. Blockbuster films still dominate when they come to the small screen and the top ten films shown on TV during the eighties have some mouth-watering audiences ranging from 18.5 million to 23.5 million (Table 3.2). James Bond is still the perennial favourite, occupying five of the top ten films by year, although judging by the performance of *Crocodile Dundee* and the two Indiana Jones' films it will be very interesting to see the results when *Crocodile Dundee II* and *Indiana Jones and the Last Crusade* hit the TV screen.

The growth of access to satellite channels may yet impact on viewing levels. Viewers in cable and satellite households spend about 7 per cent more time watching television than the average household, though this is partly because they were heavier viewers before acquiring the new channels.

THE NEED FOR AUDIENCE MEASUREMENT

What is a rating?

Ratings are the main currency for the measurement of television audiences. A television programme's rating is the size of its audience expressed as a percentage of the relevant population size. For example, the 'Adults rating for *Coronation Street* in Midlands' is the proportion of all the adults in the Midlands ITV Area who watched (a particular episode of) *Coronation Street*. In fact, this definition requires two refinements. First, the 'relevant' population is those adults living in private households capable of receiving the Central ITV station. Second, the audience size

Table 3.1 Top 10 programmes (individuals): 1980 and 1989

Position	1980 Programme	Month	Audience (millions)	Position	1989 Programme	Month	Audience (millions)
1	Live and Let Die	Jan.	23.50	1	Crocodile Dundee	Dec.	21.77
2	Dallas	Nov.	21.60	2	Only Fools & Horses	Dec.	20.12
3	To the Manor Born	Nov.	21.55	3	Coronation Street	Mar.	19.01
4	This is Your Life	Jan.	19.75	4	Blind Date	Nov.	16.86
5	My Wife Next Door	Jan.	19.75	5	Bread	Dec.	16.51
6	Jim'll Fix It	Feb.	19.20	6	Night of Comic Relief	Mar.	15.95
7	Mastermind	Nov.	19.15	7	Forever Green	Mar.	15.75
8	Blankety Blank	Dec.	19.05	8	Eastenders	Feb.	15.56
9	Coronation Street	Dec.	19.00	9	Inspector Morse	Jan.	15.49
10	Morecambe & Wise	Oct.	18.65	10	The Man with the Golden Gun	Nov.	15.47

Table 3.2 Top 10 films shown on TV and top films by year: 1980–9

Position	Top 10 films shown on TV Film	Year	Audience (millions)	Top films by year Film	Year	Audience (millions)
1	Live and Let Die	1980	23.50	Live and Let Die	1980	23.50
2	Jaws	1981	23.25	Jaws	1981	23.25
3	The Spy Who Loved Me	1982	22.90	The Spy Who Loved Me	1982	22.90
4	Diamonds Are Forever	1981	22.15	Superman	1983	16.75
5	Crocodile Dundee	1989	21.77	Raiders of the Lost Ark	1984	19.35
6	Raiders of the Lost Ark	1987	19.35	From Russia With Love	1985	17.25
7	Indiana Jones & the Temple of Doom	1987	18.95	You Only Live Twice	1986	17.30
8	Force 10 from Navarone	1982	18.90	Indiana Jones & the Temple of Doom	1987	18.95
9	Rollercoaster	1981	18.85	For Your Eyes Only	1988	17.80
10	Paint Your Wagon	1980	18.45	Crocodile Dundee	1989	21.77

and rating vary throughout the duration of the programme and is nowadays measured for each individual minute; so the minute-by-minute ratings are averaged over the whole of the programme. When this is done, a rating of 37 per cent would be typical for this perennial favourite. Some call this 37 'rating points'. Others abbreviate 'television rating' to TVR, especially in tables.

Ratings are also calculated for advertisements; in this case it is the rating of the minute in which the advert starts. Advertisers and their agencies then add these ratings over all the 'spots' (airings) of a given advertising campaign; the sum is either called the Total TVR or the Gross Rating Points (GRP). The total TVR is no longer a true percentage since it can exceed 100, but it is nevertheless a measure of the 'weight' of the advertising campaign.

If we add the audience sizes themselves rather than the corresponding TVRs, we get the total 'impacts' for the campaign. While 200 total TVRs in the North-West would imply an equal weight of advertising as 200 total TVRs in Yorkshire, the former will deliver about 10 per cent more impacts because the population of the North-West is larger by this amount. The North-West spots will therefore cost the advertiser about 10 per cent more (putting aside other factors).

Users and uses

The main user-groups for television audience ratings are:

- the broadcasters,
- the advertisers,
- the advertising agencies and media specialists.

Broadcasters encompass the BBC, the ITV companies, GMTV, Channel 4, British Sky Broadcasting and other satellite channels. All share the need for programme ratings, that is, they need to know what proportion of the population watch each of their programmes, and the regional and demographic characteristics of each audience. Not all programmes are required to achieve large audiences, but there is an expectation depending on the programme type and its place in the schedule against which actual performance can be judged.

Commercial broadcasters also require spot ratings (the rating of each commercial) and break ratings (for each commercial break) as a guide for selling commercial air-time to advertisers. Highly rated spots can be sold for a higher price and each broadcaster issues a rate-card giving the price of each spot. This will depend on the month and day-part in which it falls, and several prices will generally be quoted, each of which pre-empts any lower price already offered by another advertiser. There are also various discounts for volume, regional share and so on.

Actual expenditure is commonly expressed as cost per thousand viewers (CPT) for comparative purposes. It varies by day-part and region according to demand, being typically highest in peak-time and in the southern ITV areas. The actual selling process is increasingly handled by air-time sales houses, which depend on detailed audience measurement data.

While media owners everywhere are the driving force behind the provision of media usage data, since such data are their primary tool for selling space or time to advertisers, advertisers in turn need proof that their advertising budgets are being spent effectively. Thus the first requirement is information on the size, frequency of exposure, and demographic profile of the audience to their advertisements. Equally important is information on the cost per thousand delivered audience.

The advertiser's agency will normally provide this feedback and will then buy the air-time on behalf of the advertiser; a full-service agency will also make the advertisement, while a media specialist does not.

Agencies will typically agree with the advertiser:

- the target audience category,
- the level of expenditure on a brand over a nominated campaign period,
- the geographical dispersion (each ITV area must be bought separately).

Thus the target audience for toothpaste may be housewives, and for lager, men aged 18–34. The total expenditure will depend on the required duration and intensity of the campaign. The agency will examine relevant historical data on audience size and air-time costs to arrive at the expected number of impacts. The latter may, in turn, be broken down as the anticipated coverage (per cent of target population seeing at least one spot) multiplied by the average frequency (average number of spots seen by these viewers). All ITV areas may receive equal weight or, for instance, advertising may be concentrated in areas where the brand sells particularly well. These elements form the basis of the TV part of any media plan.

The agency must next determine which spots to employ to achieve this plan and offer to buy them. Again audience data are required at this stage. Just as the broadcaster wishes to sell each spot at the highest possible price, so the agency wishes to buy at the lowest possible price. Agencies have historically calculated the Station Average Price by dividing the monthly revenue published by the broadcaster by the total audience ('impacts') achieved, giving a *de facto* cost per thousand. The aim is then to discount below this as much as possible. Recently, however, some broadcasters have tried to move the emphasis away from discounts by withholding monthly revenue figures.

Not only are deals struck on the basis of past data and likely audience size, but the achieved audience is then examined to determine whether the campaign has delivered the expected audience. While each agency will report on its own performance on the brand, organisations such as Media Audits may also be contracted by advertisers to provide comparative data on different agencies' performance.

A number of research agencies provide supplementary services which examine the effectiveness of advertising. The impact of advertising on sales and profit cannot be measured directly, but a number of different approaches may provide valuable insights. A common measure is the awareness of the brand and attitudes towards it among the public. Either a dedicated pre-campaign/post-campaign survey may be carried out to assess changes in awareness, or this may be measured on an ongoing monitoring vehicle, of which the largest is operated by Millward Brown (see Kent, 1993). Audience data are then matched with awareness levels; experience with many previous campaigns has allowed statistical models to be built against which performance can be judged.

A similar modelling approach may also be performed, but using brand sales data rather than awareness. This task is at least as difficult due to the presence of the many other factors which affect sales – distribution levels of the product in the retail trade, 'below-the-line' activity such as discounting and other sales promotion, competitors activity and so on. Nevertheless, econometric models can achieve useful results.

Other data requirements

While ratings and commercial impacts are the day-to-day currency of the industry, the viewing data may be analysed or presented in several other ways for specific purposes. Some examples are:

• average daily or weekly hours of viewing,
• channel shares (of total viewing),
• channel reach (or patronage) – the percentage of individuals who tune into the channel at least once, for say 15 minutes minimum over a week,
• frequency of viewing to a series or advertising campaign,
• the proportion of viewing which is attributed to guests,
• the proportion of viewing attributed to replay of recorded material on VCRs, to replay of pre-recorded (bought or rented) videotapes.

In addition, information is required about the universe or television-receiving population, for example:

• universe sizes – the number and nature of the households receiving television in each broadcast area and the demographic profile of the residents,
• channel penetration – the proportion and characteristics of households in each area capable of receiving each channel.

Universe information is also required by the research suppliers in order to ensure that the viewing panels are representative of their respective populations, and to allow calculation of the appropriate processing weights. This type of information is provided by 'establishment surveys'. These surveys are described in a later section.

THE AUDIENCE MEASUREMENT INDUSTRY

Background

The development of the television broadcasting industry, which has already been described briefly, has required audience measurement to develop apace, both to cope with the increases in number of broadcasters and channels and to provide data of increasing detail and sophistication as the competition for share of audience intensifies. The roots of television audience measurement are in the earlier surveys of the radio audience, but the popularity of television with the public and hence also with advertisers meant that the funding and sophistication of this measurement soon overtook that for radio.

The earliest television audience surveys were conducted by the BBC, and these continued well after the adoption of metered panels by ITV in 1956 – in fact until 1981, when the BBC joined with ITV in using meter panels for audience data. During this period, the BBC's own Broadcasting Research Department used street-interviews to elicit day-after recall of television viewing, while ITV's data needs were supplied by TAM (Television Audience Measurement Ltd) a company jointly owned by Attwood Statistics Ltd and the AC Nielsen Co. It ran regional panels of households that were equipped with meters (the Tammeter) and which monitored the television sets, while household members were each required to complete a weekly viewing diary.

Thus for about 25 years there were two simultaneous continuous audience measurement vehicles, which, not surprisingly, produced different figures. The impetus for change was perhaps diminished by the fact that the BBC surveys generally produced higher BBC shares of audience than did the TAM panels.

In 1968 AGB, the largest market research company in the UK, now one arm of Taylor Nelson AGB, secured the measurement contract and continued with a meter and diary system until 1984.

Both the Tammeter and the AGB Setmeter used probes into each TV set to detect its on/off status and the channel tuned. These data were recorded onto heat-sensitive tape together with the time and the identity of the household.

Information on the actual audience was obtained from viewing diaries maintained by each person aged 4 and over in the panel households. Each diary spanned one week, and contained quarter-hour grids throughout each day's transmission times. The panel-member marked through each quarter hour in which they viewed for eight or more minutes.

The meter tape and the diaries were returned at the end of each week. The tapes were read by a special encoder and latterly the diaries were input to the computer using an Optical Mark Reader. In 1984 the Setmeter and diary system was replaced by a new measurement using the AGB people-meter, which in a developed form continues to be used today.

BARB

The original Joint Industry Committee for Television Audience Research (JICTAR) was replaced in 1981 by the Broadcasters' Audience Research Board (BARB). BARB is a private limited company of which the BBC and ITVA each own 50 per cent. It has a board of directors drawn from the two shareholders, the IPA and Channel 4 under an independent chairman, currently Sir Giles Shaw, MP. It employs an executive body/secretariat under the Chief Executive, Bob Hulks and a Technical Director, Tony Twyman (who is a contributor to this volume). Two principal committees report to the Board: the Audience Appreciation Management Committee and the Audience Measurement Management Committee. The AMMC includes representatives from the BBC and ITVA as well as Channel 4 and S4C, the satellite broadcasters, the Institute of Practitioners in Advertising (IPA), representing the advertising agencies, the Incorporated Society of British Advertisers (ISBA) and the Association of Media Independents (AMI).

Like JICTAR before it, BARB's function is to draw up specifications for research programmes, to award these to a research contractor, usually by competitive tender, and to oversee the contractor in the execution of its duties. BARB also collects the funding for the research from the appropriate data-users and pays the contractors. BARB has sole copyright in the audience measurement data and reports.

The 1991 BARB contract

BARB issued a specification for the 1991 contract in early 1989. Its emphasis was the provision of a measurement system which would cope with the rapid expansion in the number of channels and other viewing options, such as VCR, through the 1990s. This challenge was to be met both by suitable electronic meters and by a large and optimally structured sample capable of measuring more fragmented audiences in more detail than previously.

Contracts were awarded to run for seven years from August 1991 to two research contractors: RSMB Television Research, a subsidiary of Millward Brown, and AGB Television, a division of Taylor Nelson AGB plc.

RSMB is responsible for the sample design and control systems; it also conducts the establishment surveys, selects panel homes and recruits them. It monitors panel member compliance and contacts panel homes by telephone as necessary to maintain full co-operation. AGB is responsible for the design, supply and installation of the metering equipment. It polls each household's meters nightly to retrieve the viewing information. It monitors the performance of the metering equipment and its field engineers visit panel homes at intervals to install meters on new televisions or VCRs or to rectify any faults. AGB also processes the viewing and transmission data and provides the various forms of data output. As will be obvious, the two companies work closely together to enable the entire research process to operate smoothly.

THE RESEARCH PROCESS

This section describes each of the major components of the system by which audience estimates are produced.

Definition of viewing

Viewing of television does not necessarily require the viewer's complete concentration. People engage in a number of activities while in a room where a TV set is on, including conversation and reading, which may share the viewer's attention. One obvious reason for this is where a programme has been selected by one of the household members, but it is of lesser interest to other members who may nevertheless remain in the room. In this situation, it is necessary to provide respondents with a workable definition of whether they should consider themselves to be viewers. There are two possible approaches. One is simply to allow panel members to decide for themselves. The other is to define a viewer as any person who is present in a room where a TV set is switched on. While the latter definition is less subject to personal interpretation by panel members, it is likely that some will choose to decide for themselves anyway; it also begs the question of the definition of a room in an open-plan dwelling. Nevertheless, it is the definition adopted in the UK. The former definition is used by Nielsen in the USA.

At first sight, it might appear that TV viewing is a remarkably uniform phenomenon which would not require large sample sizes to measure with reasonable precision. After all, a person can only be in one of a few 'states': either not watching or watching one of a limited number of channels. Further, inspection of the audience size and rankings of the most popular programmes shows little variation from week to week other than due to seasonality.

This view is simplistic and in fact viewing of television is a highly variable phenomenon on several dimensions. At the broadest level, the *amount* of viewing in say a week varies greatly between individuals, from nothing to as much as 70 or 80 hours. While some of this variation can be accounted for by regional and demographic factors, which can be incorporated as strata in the sample design, there is still large variation within any one stratum. Second, any one individual does not view the same amount in successive weeks, though there is obviously a positive correlation which the use of a panel sample benefits from. Third, the division of these viewing levels between channels is obviously capable of great variation. In so far as these are largely driven by different programme preferences, there is then much variation between individuals as to *when* they view and *what* they view.

The final view is therefore one of a population which displays great variation in behaviour at all levels. Further, viewing estimates are routinely required not just for the whole population, but for a large number of demographic subgroups within each ITV and BBC area. This places considerable demands on sample sizes and is one reason why these have grown steadily over time.

Establishment surveys

These surveys have three purposes:

- To provide information on the size and structure of TV-owning households, their members and the TV-related equipment they own. Apart from the value of these data in their own right, they also provide grossing-up factors for turning panel viewing into audience estimates for the population.
- To enable these population data to be used to define appropriate control strata for the panel sample, and to calculate stratum sample sizes (target cell sizes).
- To provide a pre-surveyed bank of households (the potentials file) which can be approached throughout the year to recruit households with required characteristics to the panel.

Thus establishment surveys are an integral part of the research process.

Sample design

During the 1984–91 BARB contract each survey was designed to deliver approximately 20,000 household interviews, and was conducted each March. For the 1991–8 contract the sample size is 40,000 households and interviewing is necessarily spread throughout the year. The annual sample is selected as twelve representative replicates, which are issued as four-weekly waves of fieldwork starting in mid-January, thus missing out the Christmas/New Year period.

The establishment survey universe is all permanent residents in private households in the UK. This excludes about 3 per cent of the population who reside in non-private households (student accommodation, retirement homes, etc.) The unit of sampling is private households, with one interview per household. The sample design employs extensive stratification with geographical disproportionality, the UK being divided into geographical building blocks or strata defined by the intersection of ITV Areas and BBC Regions, some 58 in all. Minimum sample sizes for individual building blocks or groups of building blocks are set; for example, the minimum sample size for any whole ITV area (other than the Channel Islands) is 1,000 achieved interviews. In general, overlaps are sampled at about twice the rate of non-overlap ('core') areas to take account of the greater variability in viewing in overlaps arising from the greater choice of channels (though this may shortly change) and a sample of at least 100 dual/multi-ITV station homes is taken within each ITV area sample.

Within each building block, the issued household sample is derived from the Small User Postal Address File (PAF). The PAF is the Post Office's computerised list of all 'delivery points' in the UK together with their postcode. It is divided into large users, principally businesses and other institutions, which merit their own postcode, and small users, principally private dwellings, which do not. Small businesses are also presented on the small user file but are flagged as such whenever possible. Multiple household dwellings, often rented accommodation, are not separately listed and must be identified and dealt with at the interview stage.

The hierarchical structure of the postcode lends itself well to a variety of multi-stage sample designs. The establishment survey employs the postcode sector at the first stage (an example sector is HA5 4) and selects the required number of these in each building block with probability proportional to size (PPS), size being defined as the number of delivery points. A fixed number of addresses are then selected using systematic random sampling from each such postal sector.

The questionnaire

Respondents are interviewed at home by interviewers from Research Services Ltd and Millward Brown Ltd. The questionnaire covers four main areas of enquiry:

- ownership of television sets and related equipment,
- station reception capability and quality,
- current 'claimed' viewing level and station shares for the respondent and (except in one person households) claimed viewing and channel shares for the whole household,
- household demographic information.

Weighting

In outline, the achieved interview sample is weighted to targets for the number of households of size 1 (one household member) versus two or more, with further correction for the average size of household for the latter group; the exact method is detailed in the BARB Reference Manual. The targets are themselves projections for each ITV and BBC area based on OPCS information.

Reporting

Two printed reports are produced, one for ITV Areas and the other for BBC Regions; both give Network figures also. Each provides key statistics about the demographic and ownership profile of each area. More detailed breakdowns have been produced each year as a 'TAPS' report (Television Area Population Statistics). A data-tape of the individual responses and their weights is also created to enable further *ad hoc* analyses to be produced.

The AGB peoplemeter

The meter in use for the current (1991–8) BARB contract is called the AGB 4900 peoplemeter. It provides a number of capabilities not present on the previous 4800 series meter which was used for the 1984–91 BARB contract.

The 4900 meter system consists of three hardware components:

- a Meter Display Unit (MDU),
- a remote-control handset,
- a Central Data Storage Unit (CDSU).

There is an MDU for each of the television sets in the home. This is a box measuring about 8 by 4 by 2 inches which normally sits on top of the set. Its front panel contains a sixteen-character display, which is used to display messages and information to the panel members. The MDU is mains-powered and provides a 240v outlet into which the TV set is plugged. In this way, it is impossible for the MDU to be turned off while the set is on. Into the back panel of the MDU are plugged one or more 'probes', one for the television set itself and one for each attached VCR, satellite receiver or cable receiver. These probes are placed in such a position inside each piece of equipment so as to detect its on/off status and the channel to which it is tuned. The VCR probe provides further information which is described below.

The MDU has a dedicated processor with custom software, an internal clock and a memory. It continuously interrogates each probe and stores any changes of state in the memory together with the date and time.

Also associated with each MDU is a remote-control handset. This can be set at installation to communicate with the MDU using either infra-red or ultrasound to prevent interference with any existing remote controls. Its keypad contains buttons numbered 1 to 8. Members of the household are assigned their own number and their name is written on a space next to the button. In order to indicate that they have started to view, panel members press their button. The MDU confirms this action by displaying that number on its display. The number continues to be displayed until either the set is turned off or the member indicates that they have stopped viewing by pressing their number on the handset again. The MDU again records these changes of state in its memory.

Each MDU thus keeps a complete record of who is viewing and the status of all the viewing equipment, in the form of changes of status or 'switching statements'.

A single Central Data Storage Unit (CDSU) is installed in each household. It measures about 8 by 6 by 2 inches. It is located in an inconspicuous position such as behind furniture and ideally panel members need never be aware of it. Like the MDU it is mains-powered and contains a dedicated micro-processor, clock and memory; it also contains a modem and is located near a telephone point into which it is permanently plugged.

The CDSU acts as the focal point for all the MDUs in the home. It communicates with the MDUs via the domestic mains supply, thus requiring no dedicated connections to be made. It interrogates each MDU on a regular basis and copies all switching statements into its own memory.

Between 1 a.m. and 5 a.m. each night, the CDSU is itself interrogated by means of a telephone call from the AGB central computer in London (the telephone ringing is suppressed), and the information in its memory is uploaded. The call is also used to check the time on the CDSU's clock and to reset any small amount of drift; this in turn is passed to each MDU. The start and end of British Summer Time is notified in the same way. Finally, the call may be used to download any further information from the centre to govern the behaviour of the meter system. One example would be to include changes to the prompts which the MDUs display.

The entire system is designed to prevent loss of data in the face of a variety of electronic failures. For example, if problems with the telephone line prevent the CDSU from being polled on a given night, the CDSU retains its information, and several days of information can be collected in arrears. While these 'late' data clearly cannot be included in overnight reports, they can still be included on the final databases for subsequent analysis.

The CDSU also includes battery back-up to guard against mains power failures or against being unplugged and it records the timing of all such interruptions. Power failures normally mean that there will have been no TV viewing, but if the CDSU is simply unplugged, the MDUs will wait until it is reconnected and pass the backlog of switching statements to it at that time.

The probe placed inside a VCR has to monitor a wide range of conditions. It therefore contains its own micro-processor and is termed the Smartprobe by AGB. It provides not only the channel to which the VCR is tuned, but also whether the VCR is playing a tape, recording, in pause, search or fast-wind mode.

The Smartprobe also enables the identity of any material which was recorded off-air to be established at the time of play-back, so that time-shifted viewing can be included on the databases and, if desired, be included in audience estimates.

This is achieved by writing an invisible code or 'fingerprint' onto any recording which is made. This code includes the channel from which the recording is being made and the time and date of recording, on a continuous basis. When the tape is replayed, the Smartprobe looks for its own fingerprint. If none is present, this signifies that the tape has been bought or rented. If the fingerprint is found, the channel and date/time are passed to the MDU. The AGB computer subsequently matches these records against programme logs to establish exactly what material was being replayed.

The rules for inclusion of such time-shift viewing in audience estimates are described later.

The viewing panels

The measurement of the television audience is based on panel samples. This was not always the case and it is not the case for radio and print media research, so it is worth noting the advantages of a panel for television audience research. They are not dissimilar to the advantages that panels offer for consumer market research.

First, panels offer the ability to employ more sophisticated data-capture methods than could be achieved by a sequence of one-off interviews. Previously by means of diaries, this is now by peoplemeter. Continuous minute-by-minute data can thus be collected.

Second, trends and changes in viewing behaviour, audience size and so on are measured with lower sampling variation on a continuous sample, compared to the disruptive effect that the use of a series of different samples would have.

Third, data can be observed continuously for individual respondents, allowing a range of analyses such as the reach and frequency of viewing to an advertising campaign, the extent of repeat-viewing to successive episodes of a programme, and the extent of duplication of audiences between different programmes and channels.

In setting up a panel, the same elements of sample design procedures pertain as for a single-interview study. However, in other respects panels differ from *ad hoc* research. Recruitment is more complex, while panels require ongoing controls designed to ensure that the stratum samples sizes are maintained over time in the face of losses from the panel, which may be for a variety of causes. Controls may also be put in place either to increase or decrease the level of panel turnover to a desirable level. Panels also require careful management and quality control to ensure that controls are adhered to and error rates are minimised, while panel turnover and rotation need to be monitored.

Sample design

The BARB panel is in fact a collection of separate regional samples (except as qualified below), each drawn from and designed to represent a single ITV Area. The relevant population is all those households within the agreed boundary of the ITV Area that can actually receive the home ITV station. The main exclusion consists of homes near the edge of an area, probably in the overlap with another ITV Area, which can only receive ITV from that other Area. Individuals aged 4 and over in these households form the viewing base.

Like earlier JICTAR and BARB panels, the sample sizes are not directly proportional to the population sizes of the Areas. If this were done, the panel size in the smaller (i. e. less populated) Areas would be insufficient for reporting ratings at the required level of precision. Instead, the samples in the smaller Areas represent a higher proportion of their respective populations than those in the larger Areas, though they are still smaller samples in absolute terms. The current sample sizes, in numbers of households, are shown in Table 3.3, adding to 4,435 nationally. In addition, each has a 'margin' of an extra 6 per cent to allow for withheld homes and so on, giving a gross sample of 4,700.

Although the regional samples are separate, some of them overlap geographically because the ITV Areas overlap. Thus in the Midlands/Anglia overlap there will be some panel homes in the Midlands sample and some in the Anglia sample. Some of these will be dual-channel homes, that is, capable of receiving ITV from both Areas. Although the people-meter in these homes will record tuning to either station, only the tuning to the home transmitter will be used for reporting. Since each Area has its own sample, such data from adjacent samples is not needed for reporting. However, this situation leads to the possibility of using some or all of the dual-channel homes in an overlap as so-called dual-panel or

Table 3.3   Sample sizes by ITV areas

ITV Area	Households
London	475
Midlands	500
North-West	450
Yorkshire	400
Tyne-Tees	270
Central Scotland	300
Grampian	200
West	200
Wales	200
South	295
South-East	155
Anglia	400
South-West	250
Ulster	200
Border	100
Channel Islands	40

dual-reporting homes; that is, homes which form part of both Area samples. The research contractor has some freedom as to how many, if any, such homes to nominate as dual reporters. There is clearly some saving in cost because the overall number of actual homes is reduced. On the other hand, demographic control of each panel becomes harder since new dual-reporting homes must meet two sets of demographic requirements simultaneously. Currently there are approximately 100 dual-panel homes nationally.

Recruitment and installation of equipment

Once the types of homes required to join the panel have been identified, the address bank obtained from the most recent Establishment Survey (the 'potentials' file) is scanned for eligible households. These are listed and issued to the appropriate interviewers for attempted recruitment. The interviewer calls on the household and invites them to join the panel, taking care to ensure that the task required of each member is fully understood.

The rewards or 'incentive scheme' is also explained. The co-operation of panel-members is best achieved by a combination of material rewards and by instilling a sense of the usefulness of the panel-members' involvement. The need to ensure a representative sample is explained, while the value of each person's views in guiding broadcasting policy is emphasised. The rewards typically consist of a monthly prize-draw with a mixture of both large and small prizes and a six-monthly award of store vouchers. There is also a monthly newsletter with announcements about prizes and prize-winners, reminders or information relevant to the respondent's tasks, and other features of general interest such as recipes.

Once the household has agreed to join the panel, an appointment is made for an AGB installation engineer to call. He assesses the equipment to be monitored and orders the appropriate meters from head office. He also determines how the connection to the telephone line will be made and whether a visit is required by a British Telecom engineer to fit an additional connection point.

Households without a telephone require additional steps. AGB arranges for a telephone line to be installed by BT and pays any deposits, installation costs and line charges. Telephones are not provided, but the household may fit these themselves and take over the line charges at any time.

The installation engineer returns to install the metering equipment, which typically takes a half-day. This is then checked, as is the polling link by performing a 'line-test'. Finally he ensures that the names of each household member are written on the handset and that the use of the equipment is understood.

Demographic controls

Each area sample is controlled primarily by a 24–cell matrix of household types. The exact definitions of the cells, which were developed by RSMB to offer good discrimination on viewing behaviour, are very detailed and can be obtained from the BARB Reference Manual. In outline, they are constructed by interlacing three dimensions :

- household lifestage (pre-family, family, post-family with economically active adults, post-family with no economically active adults),
- socio-educational status of the head of the household,
- household size whose cell definitions vary according to household lifestage.

The required number of households in each cell is calculated from the establishment survey, together with a tolerance level either side. The aim is to keep the actual number of installed households within tolerance and as close to the target as possible.

Further control of each cell is made by recruiting homes so that the mean claimed viewing level for the cell is maintained against a target also derived from the establishment survey. This control is extremely important. Without it, there would be a tendency for the panels to under-represent light viewers of television, which would inflate the estimates of hours-of-viewing and also lead to a distortion in programme ratings towards those favoured by heavy viewers. The principal reason for this tendency is that light viewers tend to be less interested in television generally and are therefore less inclined to join the viewing panel.

In practice, balancing each panel perfectly on all the control cells is impossible due to the unpredictability of which homes will next drop out, which homes nominated as replacements will co-operate, and how long the recruitment and installation process will take. However, modest deviations of the panel profile from the targets have a negligible effect on the accuracy of the viewing figures, especially as corrective weighting is also used.

While regional disproportionality is quite common in nation-wide samples, the BARB panel is somewhat unusual in also employing demographic disproportionality. The motivation is the same: to deliver enhanced sample sizes for commonly analysed audience subgroups. Although each advertiser's target groups do differ, there is overall emphasis on the younger sections of the population – children, young adults and housewives with children. The actual method employed is to under-represent by two-thirds the last two of the 24 cells, the so-called 'C2DE early inactives'. These are post-family households of C2DE social grade whose head is an early school-leaver and with no economically active adults.

Panel master file

Running a panel requires considerable attention to be paid to maintaining accurate records about each panel home. The panel master file lies at the heart of the panel management and data-processing system. A range of information is required to ensure that a household's contribution to the output data is complete and correct, including:

- demographic characteristics – the number and identity of the household members, which can change over time, as well as data such as occupational status,
- television equipment – the number of TV sets and VCRs, a new (or disposed of) satellite dish or cable convertor, and any changes to cable channel subscriptions,

- changes to reception capability – e.g. the building of Canary Wharf cast a 'shadow' over a sizeable area roughly based on the Lea Valley. New satellite channels also impact on homes with dishes.

Each such change requires, at the least, a master file update, and may require a visit by the installation engineer, such as to monitor a new TV set. The panel master file also records which universes each home belongs to and the reporting status of the home (running-in, suspended, live, etc).

Panel turnover and rotation

Up to 25 per cent of panel homes will typically leave the panel in any year, for a variety of reasons. Households which are moving home will normally be required to leave the panel (unless they are staying within the sampling point). Other households choose to leave because changes in personal circumstances make it inconvenient to continue, or because they simply tire of continuing. Some households may be discarded because their co-operation with the data-collection process is unsatisfactory (in that they are not recording their viewing properly via the peoplemeter) or because there is an excess of homes in one of the control cells.

In addition to these causes, it is possible to operate a system of 'forced rotation' which artificially maintains turnover rates at some higher level. This is not BARB policy, though there has been some discussion of its merits, which is reported later.

Quality control, data validation and editing

The quality of each panel member's ongoing response is the subject of many check procedures. At the broadest level, there are two types of response error: technical and behavioural. The former arise through a fault in the monitoring equipment (or its installation), while the latter arise through incorrect usage of the equipment by panel members. The role of the quality-control procedures is to try to identify all such errors from ongoing examination of the resulting viewing statements, and to correct them as quickly as possible.

Certain checks are straightforward and point directly to specific types of error. For example, if a meter reports a television set having been tuned to an invalid channel (one not corresponding to a transmitter in that area), then an engineer may need to call to check the installation. Such a condition often results from the panel member having moved a television or VCR and disturbing the meter probes.

Checks are also made for television sets which have not been used for a number of weeks, and for panel members which have not reported any viewing for some time. The cause of these conditions may be technical or behavioural, or a mixture of the two. The first stage is usually to telephone the home and try to establish whether there is an obvious explanation. A set may be out of use because it has broken down, but it could also be because a new set has been acquired and viewing has transferred to it. An appropriate engineer's call is required in each case.

Similarly, a nil-viewer may have left the household, or it may be that they have simply forgotten to press their button on the handset. In the former case, a master file update is required, whereas in the latter case appropriate 're-education' is carried out over the telephone.

Checks of the nature described above help ensure that consistent data quality is maintained over time, but they take place too slowly to impact on each day's reported results directly. Each day's viewing statements are therefore also put through a 'validation' routine, which filters out any unusable data (such as invalid channels). In part this is done by rejecting the complete household from the sample for that day. However, certain edits are also applied to accepted data. These relate to so-called periods of 'uncovered tuning', or 'tuning without viewing'.

Uncovered tuning denotes that a television set is switched on but no viewers have logged in on the handset. There are four such conditions:

- leading gaps – where a set is turned on but there is a delay before the first viewing logs in,
- trailing gaps – where the last viewer departs some time before the set is switched off,
- embedded gaps – where all viewers leave for a period but one or more later logs in again,
- total (or simple) gaps – where no viewer logs throughout an entire period of tuning.

Leading gaps are not uncommon and are often brief, resulting from the need for the viewer to locate the handset and log in. In order to acknowledge that 'presence in the room' necessarily precedes logging in, BARB editing rules allow the log-in time of the first viewer(s) to be brought forward for a maximum of two minutes, providing the leading gap was not longer than five minutes. A similar rule operates for trailing gaps, and for the start and end of embedded gaps, though clearly a total gap is not edited as no viewers are associated with it.

If any uncovered tuning remains after these edits, it is then dropped from the data file. Thus it is implicitly assumed that there really are no viewers for these periods, as is often the case. Sets are left on for all sorts of reasons, such as security, to amuse babies and toddlers under the age of 4, or even for the dog.

The research day

Polling and processing of viewing statements is carried out on a daily basis. Since polling starts each night at 1 a.m., the research day is defined as running from 1 a.m. to 1 a.m. A home which is polled later than 1 a.m. may exhibit viewing statements which have occurred since 1 a.m.; these are 'put aside' for a day and then appended to the viewing statements collected the following day.

In this situation there could be confusion as to whether a programme indicated on the database as starting at say 3 a.m. on 18 January actually aired on 18 January or on 19 January. To prevent this, programme times between midnight and 5:59 a.m. are given as 2400–2959 so that 2430 on 18 January is unambiguously the morning of 19th January.

Persistence and minute attribution

Viewing statements from the peoplemeters are timed to the nearest second. This is electronically convenient, but should not be taken to imply that the data should be interpreted at this level of accuracy. Apart from the possibility of some meter clocks being a second or two adrift, the meters employ a technique called Persistence, which is best explained by example.

If a set, tuned to BBC1 for say 10 minutes, is then switched to ITV for less than 15 seconds and then back to BBC 1, the tuning to ITV is deemed too short to be material and that period will be attributed to the previous channel, BBC 1. Only when a new channel has been received for at least 15 seconds will the meter create a new switching statement, although that statement will be 'backdated' to the second in which the channel change was actually made.

The same rule is applied to viewing statements entered through the handset, that is, a viewer must have logged-in for a minimum of 15 seconds before a viewing statement is generated; as before the actual start-time is then correctly recorded.

The purpose of the Persistence rules is to prevent channel-hopping and 'grazing' from generating large numbers of switching and viewing statements which would have negligible impact on audience estimates but which could require significantly larger electronic meter memories and increased polling times.

The rule is further justified by the use of 'minute attribution' when viewing statements are processed. Since the finest unit of time for reporting purposes is the clock minute, it is necessary to have further rules to decide which channel each set is tuned to for each minute and which viewers were present for that minute. A number of alternative rules are possible, one of which is to find the channel which occupied most seconds in that minute; also to count a viewer if they viewed for at least 30 seconds. Methodological research has shown that the alternatives produce virtually identical audience estimates even for the minutes of a commercial break when switching activity tends to be higher. The current rules are:

- The channel deemed tuned for each clock minute is the one tuned for most of the minute; in this context 'set off' counts as a channel. If two or more channels are tuned for exactly equal parts of a minute then the last channel viewed is attributed to the minute.
- A viewer is deemed to have viewed for a clock minute if they viewed for the majority of the minute, that is 31 or more seconds. If they viewed for exactly 30 seconds, then the first 30–second period determines the status for the whole minute.

Programme and commercial transmission logs

All transmission events data are provided to AGB by the broadcaster responsible from their post-transmission logs and are accurate to the nearest second.

Programme data are provided as paper records; from these AGB creates electronic records which are then validated. Each record carries an AGB programme code, as well as the programme codes used in BARB's Audience Reaction service, and BARB's programme genre code. Each week approximately 16,000 programme events are processed in this way, each area and station contributing separately.

Post transmission logs of commercial events are received by AGB electronically, there being in excess of 60,000 such events per week. After validation, the data are matched with the ITVA copy clearance system so as to attach the industry-agreed product descriptions. The viewing data are then matched with the transmission logs to allow audience estimates to be calculated for each transmission.

Weighting and projection

This stage of processing attaches an appropriate weight to each viewing statement to reflect its relative contribution to audience estimates. Weights are necessary because a day's reporting sample can never be exactly representative of the population. There are three reasons why this is so:

- The panel is intentionally sampled disproportionately. Thus the groups which are over-sampled must be down-weighted and the groups which are under-sampled must be up-weighted.

- There are unintended sample imbalances arising both from the practical limitations of the panel balancing operation and from the rejection of certain homes on a daily basis because of invalid viewing data.

- Each home is actually a member of at least two and sometimes more universes. The two are its ITV Area and its BBC Region; if it can receive non-terrestrial channels it will also be in that universe.

Weighting is performed by comparing each reporting individuals' sample (such as London ITV) to the corresponding universe and computing an appropriate set of weights to bring the sample in line with the universe. In fact this requires a number of steps. The following account of these is somewhat simplified; a full account is given in the BARB Reference Manual.

Both the sample and the universe are analysed by a number of key characteristics, such as dual-ITV reception capability, and the process of 'rim-weighting' is employed to balance the sample to the universe. The resulting weights are more properly called projection factors, since they average not to one, but to the overall grossing-up factor (ratio of population size to panel size). An introductory account of rim-weighting is given by Sharot (1986) while a description of the particular rims used is given in the BARB Reference Manual.

Once rim-weighting is done, an audience estimate for a population category represented in the weighting process can be derived by multiplying the minutes of viewing on each contributing viewing statement by its weight and summing over the viewing statements. This audience estimate can in turn be expressed as a rating by dividing by the appropriate population size and multiplying by 100.

Extra processing is required for any reporting category not represented in the rim-weighting, such as AB men in a given ITV Area. The sum of the weights will not be exactly equal to the universe size for such categories. The ratio (universe/sum of weights) is calculated and applied as a further weight, or category factor, in calculating audiences for the category.

However, application of the same procedure to C1 men will result in audience figures which will not add exactly to the audience estimate for ABC1 men, a rim-weighting category. A final stage called category balancing is therefore employed, in which the excess or deficit is removed by further factoring the AB men and C1 men audiences equally so as to add to the ABC1 men audience. Similar weighting is performed for BBC Regions and for the non-terrestrial reception households.

Viewing by guests and visitors

The viewing panel would ideally capture TV viewing by panel members even outside their own homes. This is not practical with any degree of reliability or accuracy and a different approach is adopted. The major part of out-of-home viewing is in fact conducted in the homes of friends or relations. This 'universe of viewing' is sampled in a different but quite satisfactory way, by monitoring the viewing of guests and visitors in BARB panel homes. By this method, the same peoplemeters may be used to provide a reliable and reasonably accurate measure of this element of viewing.

Measurement is achieved by two methods. First, regular visitors such as relatives may be allocated a button as though they were members of the household, up to the limit of the eight available buttons. Their age and sex are recorded at the time the button is allocated to provide more detailed reporting.

Second, viewing by occasional guests and visitors is captured using further buttons on the handset. When a guest starts viewing in a panel home, they (or a member of the household familiar with the system) press the New Guest button on the handset. The display on the MDU then leads the guest through a series of questions; in its current implementation these will ask for the age and sex of the guest, though the MDU is capable of asking further information. This information is entered through the handset using the numbered buttons and a Yes and a No button.

When this is complete, the MDU allocates a free guest number to the guest, in the range G1 to G7, displays YOU ARE GUEST 2 (say) for 10 seconds, and adds G2 to the currently displayed list of viewers. By this means the MDU can cope with up to eight household members or regular guests viewing simultaneously with up to seven further guests, on each set in the home.

The CDSU remembers the details of each new guest that registers, so that if they stop viewing and later resume viewing on the same or any other set that day, they merely need to press G2 (in this case) to indicate their viewing. The meter may optionally be set to retain these details for any number of subsequent days, though this facility is not currently activated in the UK.

Guest viewing requires separate treatment in the audience calculation process. Although the meter captures the age and sex of each viewing guest, other characteristics of the guest are not known, such as whether they are a housewife. It is therefore necessary to allocate guest viewing across these population groups and this is done by assuming that the profile of guests in each minute is the same as that of the panel-member audience. For example, if 30 per cent of the panel-member audience were housewives, then 30 per cent of the guest audience is assumed to be housewives.

Consolidation of VCR play-back

As noted above, the peoplemeter places an electronic fingerprint on all material recorded off-air so that time-shifted viewing can be allocated to the appropriate transmission. This allows the time-shifted viewing to be included with the live viewing to provide a consolidated audience estimate.

The industry has adopted a standard which determines whether any particular minute of time-shifted replay is to be included in the consolidated audience estimate for that channel for that minute. The basic rule is that it is included providing the replay is within seven days of recording. It is known that the majority of material which is ever replayed (not all of it is) is in fact replayed for the first time within a week.

The rule is actually modified slightly for operational reasons, to speed up delivery of consolidated audience estimates. Only replay within 163 hours (rather than the full 168 hours) is included. This reflects the fact that the Research Day runs from 1 a.m. to 1 a.m. (start of polling). To use the 168-hour rule would mean that play-back taking place at say 2 a.m. on a Monday morning of material recorded at 2 a.m. a week earlier could not be included in the report for the week just ended without delaying the report by a further day. Under the 163-hour rule there is no need to wait the extra day as these data are not included, and the loss of audience is clearly minimal.

Out-of-universe viewing

A number of viewing situations are not covered by the BARB measurement. The measurement 'universe' is viewing made within private households. Among the areas which are excluded are viewing:

- in institutions, e. g. student residences, hospitals, retirement homes,
- in hotels, bars, shops, airports,
- to battery operated sets in any location (even, for technical reasons, within the home).

Viewing in second homes within the UK is nominally included but in practice they are unlikely to be contacted.

The total contribution of all these omissions is a modest percentage of the overall audience. Moreover, their inclusion on an ongoing basis represents a considerable research effort, the cost of which would be out of proportion to the practical value of the information gleaned. Instead, *ad hoc* studies are conducted from time to time as required.

DATA REPORTING AND AVAILABILITY

Methods of reporting

Up to 1991 audience estimates and ratings were issued on a weekly basis as a set of printed reports. Of these, the *Green Book*, which contained audiences and ratings for each channel in each ITV Area, was perhaps the most widely used. Other volumes gave audiences by BBC Region, and for commercial transmissions.

In 1991 the major part of this output was replaced by electronic reporting in the form of two different databases – Database I, which contains viewing statements and Database II, giving audience estimates. This change was made necessary by the considerable increase in the volume of output data resulting from:

- the need to report on non-terrestrial channels, which more than double the overall number of channels,
- the provision of both live (as aired) audiences and consolidated audiences (including time-shifted VCR viewing),
- the move to overnight reporting, requiring faster dissemination of data,
- an expansion in the number of audience categories reported.

A limited weekly printed report, the *ITV Network Report*, is still produced, but this is restricted to networked programmes on the four terrestrial channels. It gives for each such programme:

- live and consolidated network audience and TVRs for all individuals,
- consolidated network TVRs for adults, men, women, housewives and children,
- consolidated TVRs by ITV Area for all individuals.

In addition, there is for each quarter-hour:

- live and consolidated network TVR for all individuals and the five audience categories mentioned above.

There is also supplementary information on population and panel sizes, VCR usage, guest viewing and hours of viewing across the week. A limited report is also produced for the BBC.

Database I contains all the details of the panels characteristics and viewing that are needed to calculate audience estimates. It gives:

- panel home and member details (demographics, etc.),
- live viewing sessions and VCR recording and play-back sessions, with content identified for the latter,
- the sample weights for each day to be used in calculating audiences,
- universe sizes for converting audience sizes to ratings.

Versions are available on a daily and weekly basis. The daily file is available by electronic data transfer around midday on the day after transmission, and gives information on the prior day's viewing as well as any changes to the panel home and member details. The weekly version is available on computer tape; it includes the data in the seven daily files, a complete record of all home and member details and the universe data. A second weekly tape provides the transmission events (programmes and commercials).

Database I is provided primarily for the benefit of the various data analysis bureaux, which in turn provide processed information to data users. In particular, any analysis, such as coverage and frequency, which requires as input the viewing sessions of each individual, must be produced from Database I, as must any audience estimates not already provided on Database II.

Database II gives a range of pre-calculated audience estimates, as well as the transmission details. There are four separate files containing audiences for:

- each clock quarter-hour,

- each programme, as well as the start time, duration, title and genre classification of the programme and programme codes,
- commercial transmissions, as well as the start time and duration, product description code and product field classification,
- commercial breaks with product information.

Each file gives both live and consolidated audiences for up to 51 pre-defined audience categories for ITV Areas, the 12 non-overlapping BBC Regions and (from 1993) the seven overlapping Channel 4 'macro' regions. The VCR recording audience is also given.

Database II is released on three time-scales :

- daily via electronic data transfer, giving live audiences only for eleven audience categories for quarter hours,
- daily, eight days after the reporting day, via electronic transfer, to allow audience consolidation, for audience transmissions only,
- weekly, eight days after the reporting week, again to allow consolidation, giving all information.

Data analysis bureaux

BARB grants various forms of licence to companies which wish to provide further analysis services, the 'BARB bureaux'. The current principal bureaux are AGB and Donovan Data Systems.

AGB acts as a bureau in a separate capacity from its role as BARB research contractor. AGB is the leading supplier of on-line analysis systems with products including FACETS (campaign frequency and coverage), REACTS (analysis of advertising impacts for competing brands in a market) and Programme Profiles (programme audience demographics). It is currently developing a range of new PC-based analyses, including the AGB Optimiser, which helps agencies optimise the selection of advertising spots. The AGB bureau also produces *Trends for Television*, a monthly printed report covering key audience data used by the television industry – hours and shares of viewing, top programmes, top advertised brands and so on.

Donovan Data Systems is the major supplier of computerised administrative systems to advertising agencies. Such systems provide unified control of the various activities of an agency, from production of the commercial through to booking air-time and client billing. For some years it has also provided limited data analysis capabilities (now being expanded), while an arrangement known as the 'Donovan gateway' between

DDS and AGB has enabled agencies to access AGB's on-line analysis services through their Donovan terminal.

SUPPLEMENTARY RESEARCH

Additional panel classifications

In addition to the demographic information held for each household, a number of supplementary classifications are collected in the general area of product usage and lifestyle, for example pet ownership, credit card holding, travel abroad. At the current time, audiences for the following five classifications are available on Database II with the total of 51 categories:

* business spenders – adults aged 16 and over who spend £1,000 or more per annum on business,
* pub goers – adults aged 18 and over who go to pubs,
* dog shopper – adults aged 16 and over who do the household shopping and live in a dog-owning household,
* motorists – adults aged 16 and over who are the main driver of a car,
* adults aged 16 and over in homes with Astra satellite reception.

ITV Area boundary surveys

ITV Areas are defined in terms of a number of local authority Administrative Districts (ADs). An AD is included in an ITV Area if sufficient households in the AD receive the home ITV station for the Area. The criterion is that 15 per cent of households in the AD must pass the following test:

* the household can receive home ITV but no other ITV station, or
* the household can receive home ITV and also one or more other ITV stations, but the housewife's 'preference to view' the home station is at least two out of ten.

The 'preference to view' refers to the number of hours that the housewife claims to view home ITV out of every 10 hours of viewing of ITV as a whole.

Some ADs meet this criterion in respect of two or even three ITV Areas and are therefore included in each; thus certain adjacent ITV Areas overlap. BARB produces a map which shows the outline of each ITV Area.

The boundary of an ITV Area only changes if reception conditions change, which generally means that a transmitter change of some sort has taken place. If an ITV station believes that an AD not currently in its Area should be included, a boundary survey is conducted (usually through BARB) in the AD.

The survey is based on an unclustered sample of households across the AD in order to capture accurately any variation in reception conditions. Traditionally, a sequential sampling scheme is used. This means that if the proportion of households in the initial sample which pass the reception test is either much less than or much more than 15 per cent, then no further interviews are taken. On the other hand, if the result is close to 15 per cent, further interviews are conducted to increase the precision of the result. This is continued until there is sufficient confidence as to which side of 15 per cent the result lies.

The BBC, Channel 4 and ISBA also maintain their own regional maps.

Coincidental surveys

The term 'coincidental' is used to describe the technique of contacting a sample of households in order to establish what viewing is taking place at the very moment of contact. With the growth of telephone ownership, the telephone provides the most effective way of conducting such a survey. The clear advantage of a coincidental survey is the total avoidance of recall error together with a response rate somewhat higher than panel co-operation rates.

In order to provide a broad base of data, contacts are spread in a planned manner over the days of the week and over time of day; but even with this design, a coincidental study is not capable of providing viewing data on a minute-by-minute basis, or any data at all outside the hours considered acceptable for making contact by telephone. Thus the main role of coincidental studies nowadays is to provide validation of a diary-based measurement or peoplemeter measurement; we will discuss them in the latter context only.

The basic technique is to ask the respondent whether any television sets were turned on in the home at the moment that their telephone rang (they may have turned the set off in order to answer the telephone). For each set that is on, the respondent is asked who was watching and may be encouraged to leave the telephone in order to check. The time that the call was answered is noted, accurate to the minute.

There are two distinct ways of performing such a study. The first is to conduct the study on the panel itself while the second is to conduct a stand-alone sample. These two types of study naturally provide different insights into the validating of the panel measurement.

A 'within-panel' coincidental provides a direct measure of the accuracy of the peoplemeter as an instrument of data-capture. The responses gained from the study are compared with the peoplemeter records on a home-by-home, set-by-set and person-by-person basis for the exact minute of contact (though a one-minute tolerance is required to allow for a few seconds error by the interviewer in recording the time). For any panel-member, there are four possible outcomes:

(a) viewing, button is pressed (correct),
(b) not viewing, button is pressed (incorrect),
(c) viewing, but button not pressed (incorrect),
(d) not viewing, button not pressed (correct).

In each case the telephone response is taken as the definitive indicator of whether a person is viewing. We can assemble the frequency of these four outcomes into a table as shown in Table 3.4. From this table four different measures of accuracy can be derived:

(1) correct use of buttons among viewers
        = $100a/(a+c)$
(2) correct use of buttons among non-viewers
        = $100d/(b+d)$
(3) overall accuracy of button pushing
        = $100(a+d)/(a+b+c+d)$
(4) reported viewing index
        = $100(a+b)/(a+c)$

Table 3.4   The four possible coincidental survey outcomes

	Viewing?	
	Yes	No
Button pressed?		
Yes	a	b
No	c	d

The ideal outcome in each case is 100. Measures (1), (2) and (3) are each concerned with 'gross error', or error at the individual level. To the extent that measure (1) falls short, this shows the extent of under-reporting of viewing by viewers. The extent that measure (2) falls short gives the extent of over-reporting by non-viewers (who may have been viewing previously but omitted to log out when they stopped viewing).

Measure (3), though still a useful summary, is perhaps of lesser interest because it is affected not only by the levels of (1) and (2) but also by the rating, which varies greatly over the course of a day.

None of these three measures says anything directly about the accuracy of the audience estimates delivered by the panel. This is provided by measure (4), which measures the net error. Because gross errors encompass both over-reporting (b) and under-reporting (c), some cancellation takes place and the net error is less.

Table 3.5 shows the results for all panel members in the survey conducted in 1992. The net error in the audience estimate is very small indeed.

Table 3.5 Coincidental survey results, 1992 (%)

	Viewing?	
	Yes	No
Button pressed?		
Yes	30.0	3.3
No	2.9	63.8

Net error = 2.9%–3.3% = –0.4%

This analysis may be conducted for subgroups of the sample, such as men, women and children, for multi-set homes, and so on. Studies like this have been conducted on the BARB panel on a near-annual basis for some years.

The second type of coincidental study is performed on a stand-alone sample. Such a study sets out to provide an estimate of the *total* error of the panel measurement, including not only errors of recording, but also sampling error, whether random or not. In order to achieve this, the coincidental study must offer substantially lower error itself, necessitating a large sample and repeated call-backs to achieve the highest possible response rate.

This type of coincidental only provides evidence about the net error. Further, the analysis of the results is complicated by the non-response, however small. Normal methods of analysis implicitly assume that non-respondents are similar to respondents; but here it is vital to distinguish between four groups:

- respondents – all at home,
- refusals – all at home,
- non-contacts – at home but did not answer,
- non-contacts – not at home.

Only the non-contacts contain a proportion of 'not-at-homes', and this reduces the viewing level among this group. Thus non-respondents overall will probably have a lower viewing level (rating) than respondents, and sophisticated analysis is called for to allow for this effect.

BARB has not commissioned a separate-sample coincidental in recent years though they have been conducted in the USA.

CURRENT TRENDS AND FUTURE DEVELOPMENTS IN TELEVISION

The television industry continues to change, and these developments place new demands on the audience research process and on users of the data. Some major changes that will continue to affect the measurement of television audiences in the 1990s are outlined in the sections below.

The growth in commercial traffic

A major effect of the launch of Channel 4 and the growth of transmission hours has been the expansion in commercial minutage available to advertisers. In 1980 this amounted to around 620 minutes per week in a typical ITV Area, and has subsequently trebled such that most areas now sell around 1,800 minutes of air-time per week. In order to do this, areas such as London carried nearly 190,000 commercials in 1989 compared to 66,000 in 1980.

Across the decade the industry has also experienced a change in the length of commercials used to fill the available air-time. The trend has been away from 15-second and 45-second commercials towards 10-, 20- and 40-second commercials, followed by the decreasing role of 30-second spots as longer spots (40 seconds +) increased in importance. These changes add considerably to the volumes of data processed and reported, and place new demands on agencies in choosing how to allocate advertising expenditure.

Satellite and cable

As noted earlier, reception of extra-terrestrial channels is currently growing fast and will probably continue to do so for some time. The three methods of receiving these channels are:

- satellite dish, also known as DTH (direct-to-home),
- broadband cable (capable of carrying several channels),
- SMATV (satellite master antenna television), which is using a single dish to serve an entire block of flats.

As at June 1993 the BARB estimate of the number of dish-owning households was 2.44 million and the number of broadband households was 784,000, with a combined annual growth rate of over 500,000. The number of SMATV households was by comparison quite small.

Thus at that time around 3.2 million households could receive satellite channels and at current growth rates this could rise to 4 million by 1994 and 5 million – nearly a quarter of households – by 1996.

This growth must be reflected by increasing numbers of cable and satellite homes on the BARB panels, which require extra metering equipment to probe the satellite receiver as well as the television sets and VCRs. The size of the master files listing the receivable channels grows as a result, as does the number of programme events which must be notified to and reported on by the research agency.

Terrestrial broadcasting

Satellite television is not alone in undergoing rapid change. All the ITV franchises were put out to tender in 1991, creating a situation where the future of BARB and therefore the BARB panel was at least in theory unsecured. In the event, four ITV companies were replaced by new ones with effect from 1 January 1993:

- Thames Television by Carlton Television in London on weekdays,
- TVS by Meridian Broadcasting in the South Area,
- TSW by West Country Television in the South West Area,
- TV-AM by GMTV (Good Morning Television) for the breakfast television franchise.

Thankfully, the new encumbents picked up their BARB responsibilities with no disturbance to the research process. Channel 4 also became responsible for selling its own air-time at the beginning of 1993, creating seven new 'macro regions' to allow regional advertising as well as national.

Also in 1992 came the ITC's invitation for applications for the Channel Five licence. In the event there was only one applicant – Channel Five

Holdings – and the ITC announced in December 1992 that it was unwilling to award the licence – at least for the time being. Channel Five would have posed a particular problem for audience measurement because it was planned to transmit it on Channel 36, the frequency on which most VCR's output the signal to the television set. To receive the station at all, most VCR homes would have to retune their VCR and television, in turn requiring recalibration of the metering equipment in panel homes.

Television technology

Televisions continue to benefit from advances in electronic design and manufacturing, resulting in benefits for the consumer such as declining real prices and improved reliability. However, such changes also present a challenge to the designers of metering equipment. The number of points of access to the internal circuitry which can be 'probed' continues to shrink and new types of circuitry require new types of probe. On the other hand, the same technology is available to improve the design of meters.

Computerisation

The increase in the data-processing burden on the research agencies and data-analysis bureaux can be met through the use of increasingly powerful mainframe computers, while personal computers are able to handle larger portions of the total data-analysis requirement. PCs also allow new software to be developed to answer questions that previously could not be tackled economically, such as the optimisation of the selection of advertising spots.

Quantitative and qualitative research

At the time of the award of the 1991 contract there was much talk from some advertising agencies about the limited relevance of ratings to media buying decisions and a stated preference for qualitative research into, for example, the best 'context' (type of programme) in which to place advertisements for any given product. There is undoubtedly a role for both types of information. Nevertheless, the vast majority of agencies continue to use ratings as the final arbiter of the cost-effectiveness of their buying decisions.

Panel control

The research agencies continue to wrestle with the problems of maintaining a representative panel in a period of gradually declining co-operation rates among the general public. The 1991 panel saw a fairly widespread change to the demographic controls to be used for balancing the panel, including the introduction of a control by ethnic origin. There was at the time also some debate as to the merits of setting a minimum rate of turnover of the panel rather than permitting panel homes to stay for, potentially, the whole seven-year life of each panel.

There are two possible reasons for taking this course of action. The first is to ensure that no home is allowed to stay on the panel for more than a certain time in order to reduce the effect of gradual fatigue by panel-members in providing data. The second is to equalise turnover rates across the various control cells in order to provide better demographic control over the panel.

BARB decided against such enforced rotation because the substantial cost could not be justified given the lack of evidence that there would be a real benefit to the accuracy of the data. By contrast, however, AC Nielsen currently imposes a maximum time-in-service of two years on households on its national panel in the USA to mitigate the effects of fatigue. A discussion of these issues can be found in Sharot (1991).

On a different note, a trend which may impact on the research process in the 1990s is the gradual harmonisation of definitions and methods across Europe (see Chapter 2).

Viewing of pre-recorded tapes

As described earlier, the AGB peoplemeter's VCR fingerprinting technology allows identification of programme content for time-shifted material. All other tape replay, having no fingerprint, is ordinarily lumped together as 'uncoded play' and includes bought, rented and borrowed tapes without differentiation. In order to provide audience estimates for specific rental and sell-through titles, AGB launched a trial service in 1991 called Videotrak. Agreements were made with film distributors for a fingerprint to be applied to tapes at the bulk-copying stage. When such tapes are played in BARB panel homes, the meter detects the code in the normal way.

This system enables production of estimates of the number of homes renting each tape in each week after launch and of the size and profile of the viewing audience. For tapes containing advertisements prior to the film, minute-by-minute audiences could also be calculated to provide the impacts for each separate commercial.

Audience Reaction

In addition to the measurement of audience size, broadcasters also need to monitor what viewers think of the programmes they view. The principal source of information is the BARB Television Opinion Panel (TOP), also known as the Audience Reaction Service. The service is operated for BARB by the Broadcasting Research Department (BRD) of the BBC. Data are made available to the ITV companies and sales houses (but not to advertisers or their agencies).

The service is based on a weekly diary listing all programmes on the four terrestrial channels. A panel of 3,000 respondents aged 12 and over score each programme viewed (there is no strict definition of a viewer) on a scale from 1 to 6, as shown in Table 3.6.

Table 3.6   The BBC Audience Appreciation Index Scale

6 = extremely interesting and/or enjoyable
5 = very interesting and/or enjoyable
4 = fairly interesting and/or enjoyable
3 = neither one thing nor the other
2 = not very interesting and/or enjoyable
1 = not at all interesting and/or enjoyable

An overall programme score, its Appreciation Index (AI), is calculated as the average of the awarded scores, re-expressed as a percentage (i.e. 0 per cent corresponds to a mean of 1.0 (all 1's) and 100 per cent to a mean of 6.0 (all 6's). The AI is published if at least 25 viewers score a programme, and a demographic breakdown is provided given at least 50 viewers.

In practice, the AI for most programmes falls in the range 65 – 75. The score is not directly related to the audience size. For example, a low-appeal programme may well deliver both a small audience and a low AI, but a programme with intentional minority appeal may receive a good AI score from a relatively small audience. Menneer (1987) argues that there is no reason to expect a relationship between AI scores and audience ratings since they measure different things. Audience size for any programme is determined largely by the time of day it is broadcast and what the competing programmes are, irrespective of the quality of the programme. AIs are a crucial and necessary complement to estimates of audience size in evaluating channel and programme performance.

The AI score is a useful but crude measure of audience appreciation of a programme, and a second booklet ('Viewpoint') is placed to capture more detailed information about programmes of current interest to the broadcasters, such as new series. Questions may cover such aspects as the plot, characters, specific episodes and so on. The BBC's contract to supply audience reaction data terminates in 1994 and tenders are currently being invited from agencies to provide an enhanced, possibly electronic, service to replace TOP.

Single-source data

The term 'single-source data' is normally used to mean the collection of both media exposure and product consumption (or purchasing) from a single respondent sample. Detailed information on both aspects from a continuous panel would in principle allow direct analysis of the effect of advertising exposure on product usage. In the context of television, it would, for example, be possible to see whether those who did view an advertising campaign subsequently bought the product at a higher rate than non-viewers.

In practice, two research issues stand in the way of such a research vehicle. One is the double burden on panel-members. With electronic devices such as peoplemeters and in-home barcode scanners this is perhaps no longer insurmountable. The other problem is that the sample sizes required to permit analysis of the above sort are very large.

Single-source panels of this sort are ultimately of most interest to advertisers, who would be able to test the effect on sales of different advertising strategies. Research companies which have launched trial operations (most recently AC Nielsen's Statscan service) have not found it easy to turn in a profit from the limited number of brands which can be analysed on a panel of just a few hundred homes. The even greater costs involved in a larger panel could only be supported if the panel were also the basic vehicle for market measurement, and ideally also for audience measurement. Such a vehicle would demand extraordinary co-ordination between different research users to agree a technical specification which served everyone's needs.

Data fusion

In the face of these drawbacks, the technique of data fusion has gained some momentum in the last few years. It involves merging the data from a media panel with a product panel to create a single database simulating that from a single sample. This is done by matching each respondent from one sample with a similar respondent (in terms of key demographic and other characteristics) in the other sample. Since the sample will usually be of different sizes, some respondents in the larger sample will be matched to more than one member of the smaller sample.

Once a statistically optimised set of matches has been made, the data from one sample (the 'donor' sample) is copied across to the other sample (the 'recipient' sample), using the matches to determine which recipient(s) receive each donor's data. The recipient sample is then made available for analysis as though it were a single-source sample.

BARB has sponsored just such a fusion between the television audience measurement panel and BMRB's Target Group Index (TGI) survey. The TGI routinely collects extensive data on product consumption and usage and on exposure to all major media. As such it is a major tool for planners of advertising campaigns within advertising agencies. However, the very broad scope of the measurement necessarily limits the amount of detail in any one area; thus the information on television viewing is more akin to the 'claimed viewing' collected on the BARB Establishment Survey than to the actual Peoplemeter data.

The fusion of the two sources to provide 'Target Group Ratings' redresses this. Each six-monthly TGI sample is treated as a donor sample and the current BARB panel is the recipient sample. The two are matched and the extensive TGI data is then copied onto the BARB panel to create a fused database combining the TGI data and a history of peoplemeter data.

Because the BARB panel is the recipient sample, ratings data for standard audience categories are unaffected by the fusion, but in addition, ratings and viewing patterns may be produced for any product usage group of interest.

Passive metering

The peoplemeter system is the current state-of-the-art for the measurement of television audiences. It is much more accurate than using recall interviews or paper diaries and provides ratings at the minute-by-minute level. Nevertheless, the need for each respondent to push their button on the handset at the start of each viewing session and again at the end (unless switching off) is still a source of panel burden and reporting inaccuracy which it would be desirable to avoid.

To this end, the major ratings suppliers have for some years been trying to develop a 'passive meter' which would automatically detect who is viewing as well of course as the channel tuned. While systems have been promoted by some companies using a degree of imputation (such as based on who normally sits where when viewing), nothing less than a full recognition system is likely to prove satisfactory in practice.

The method currently most favoured by both Taylor Nelson AGB and AC Nielsen employs a set-top video-camera feeding a facial recognition computer. The computer is initially 'trained' on each panel member's face. Thereafter it compares each face that it sees to these and decides whether it is looking at a known panel member; unknown faces are assumed to be guests.

At the time of writing, development is continuing towards a system which is sufficiently accurate in the variety of home environments in which it must work, and which can be manufactured in a compact unit at a price commensurate with a peoplemeter. Nearer that time associated research issues must also be dealt with. One concern is the acceptability of the device to the public. People engage in all sorts of activities in front of their television sets; it may prove difficult to convince them that the meter does not create a photographic record. A second issue is that true second-by-second audience counts would probably show lower figures during commercial breaks than the current system, and may be unattractive to broadcasters for this reason. A passive meter is also likely to be more costly than the peoplemeter. In conclusion, it is likely that the Peoplemeter will remain the approved method of measuring television ratings into the next century.

REFERENCES

BARB Reference Manual, available from BARB, Glenthorne House, Hammersmith Grove, London W6 0ND.

Kent, R. A. (1993) *Marketing Research in Action*, London, Routledge.

Menneer, P. (1987) 'Audience appreciation – a different story from audience numbers', *Journal of the Market Research Society*, Vol. 29, No. 3.

Sharot, T. (1986) 'Weighting Survey Results', *Journal of the Market Research Society*, Vol. 28, No. 3, July.

Sharot, T. (1991) 'Attrition and rotation in panel surveys', *The Statistician*, Vol. 40, pp. 325–31.

FURTHER READING

An excellent account of the development of television broadcasting may be found in *British Television Advertising: The First Thirty Years*, ed. Brian Henry, Century Benham, London, 1986. See also: Beville, H. M., Jr, *Audience Ratings: Radio, Television and Cable*, Lawrence Erlbaum Associates, Hillsdale, New Jersey and London, 1985; Goodhardt, G. J., Ehrenberg, A. S. C. and Collins, M. A., *The Television Audience: Patterns of Viewing – An Update*, 2nd edn, Gower, Vermont, and Blackmore Press, Dorset, 1987. The periodical *Admap* has many articles on television audience research; in particular, William Phillips is a frequent contributor. *UK Media Yearbook*, 1992/93, Zenith Media, London, provides up-to-date statistics on television and other media.

Chapter 4

Measuring audiences to radio

Tony Twyman

Although radio is a broadcast medium, it presents problems for audience research which in many ways are very different from television, and which in some respects make it relatively more complex and more difficult. This chapter therefore begins with a discussion of the special nature of radio audiences. It then turns to the range of methods and techniques that can be used for measuring the size and composition of radio audiences before looking at the research evidence on how these techniques compare in practice in a number of different countries. The chapter concludes by looking in some detail at the organisation of radio research in the UK and offering some thoughts on the special requirements of radio advertising and the measurement of its effectiveness.

THE NATURE OF RADIO LISTENING

The problems that arise in the measurement of radio audiences are a result of the following features that are, of course, interrelated:

- because of the way memory works, recall of radio listening tends to be more difficult than for other media,
- it is a medium ideally suited to being used as a companion to other concurrent activities with which attention is shared,
- listeners tend to be mobile, so a lot of listening takes place outside the home, often on radios not owned by or tuned in by the listener,
- unlike television, radio programme content tends to flow continuously rather than being a series of unique broadcasts,
- radio is a highly fragmented and rapidly-expanding medium; in some countries hundreds of stations are available, and even in the UK more than 20 stations can be received in some areas,
- with many regional stations, the financial size of a typical radio station (as with local press) tends to be relatively small. This tends to restrict

the scale of research as to sample size and frequency. Even if it were practicable, metering would not be affordable.

Events are retrieved from memory only if they were stored on the way in along with some association. It is the association (sometimes called 'coding' or 'labelling') that is invoked in order to recall past events. Commonly, these associations relate to the time and place that the event occurred, to the uniqueness of the event, and to habitual behaviour. Because listeners tend to be mobile, because programmes are seldom unique, and because listening is often casual rather than habitual, the content of radio listening is often difficult to code and subsequently to retrieve. So, too, is identification of the radio station listened to (this is done automatically for television by the Peoplemeter). In some research by the Bureau of Broadcast Measurement in Canada (discussed below) only about 60 per cent of those aware that the radio was switched on felt that they knew exactly what 'the programme' was. In consequence, radio stations need to establish an identity over and above their individual programme material for people to realise that they are listening to a particular service (crucial for media research) and to develop loyalty (essential for a station's success).

In short, all the advantages of radio as a medium – that it supplements people's ongoing lives rather than requiring everything else to come to a standstill – militate against accurate recall. Furthermore, the audience to any transmission will comprise a mixture of the ways in which people are relating to the medium: those who are involved and give their full attention to the programme, those who have it merely as background, those who chose the programme purposefully and those who did not. Many will be doing housework, studying, decorating, talking and so on while the programme is broadcast. An example of the ranges of contexts in which radio is heard is provided by Day *et al.* (1984), who recorded the locations in which adults in London claimed to listen to radio before 9.00 a.m. The results are shown in Table 4.1.

RESEARCH TECHNIQUES

Research techniques vary according to a number of key dimensions:

- the criterion of 'listening' that they impose,
- how far they reduce co-operation bias and sample the entire population,
- their degree of reliance on unaided and unprompted memory,
- the mode of data capture.

Table 4.1   The early morning audience: adults 15+, London weekdays
            up to 9.00 a.m.

Occupation/location	% claiming
Lying in bed	23
Getting up	62
Having a wash or bath	38
Preparing meals	28
Eating	43
Washing up	18
Getting ready to go out	50
Driving to work	15

The first of these refers to the question: 'How seriously do I have to have been listening to count?' In the Canadian research, for example, it was found that some people thought that their listening did not count when others had chosen the programme and were in control of the set. Asking questions about other media in a survey, furthermore, seems to affect that criterion. Other media, particularly television, cinema and the press, represent much more discrete events with codable contents and more active participation. Their memory-forming capacity should be far greater and may then set higher standards of 'quality' of memory than radio can achieve.

The issue of potential co-operation bias is an important one. There is a tendency in all media research for those most readily accessible to research to be more accessible to the media. People will have an inclination not to participate in research about something they do not do very much. It therefore becomes of major importance in media research to ensure that those who are less committed to the medium are encouraged to take part, so covering as much of the population as possible and not being accidentally selective. Some of the North American media research (discussed below) is based on relatively low response rates and can suffer from co-operation bias in this way. Some important elements in any technique therefore are the mode of sampling, presentation of the task and recruitment success.

When asking people about their listening, very different results will be achieved when they are given lists of programmes that have been or will be broadcast in their area compared with being simply asked to recall unaided what programmes they listened to. Prompted lists will produce much more listening, as will the thoroughness of attempts to help respondents to reconstruct their day.

The mode of data capture is clearly of major importance in terms of what kind of radio listening is retrieved by the respondent. The major categories are:

- systematic recall,
- diaries,
- general habit questions,
- coincidental interviewing,
- recording devices.

Systematic recall

This involves asking people to reconstruct a previous period and report what listening occurred. This could be done for earlier periods on the day of interview or for several previous days. Usually, however, the method is day-after recall (DAR), and the respondent goes through the previous day and hopefully identifies the occasions and content of radio listening that took place 'yesterday'. Thus a day's data is obtained from one interview.

The interviewing can be conducted by telephone, but in the UK has usually been applied in face-to-face interviews. Variations in the technique revolve around where and how the sample is contacted and therefore what kind of sample is interviewed. Major sources of difference in the results achieved arise from variations in the degree of programme material prompting used, the trouble taken to reconstruct the previous day's activities, and the degree of station explanation, description and prompting built into the survey. The amount of aid given to identify programmes and station listened to may vary quite accidentally and affect the results. In a comparison of two surveys in Ireland, each conducted for a different station, it was found that client stations naturally and quite innocently provided better information about their own programmes than for other stations leading to better prompt aids in each case for the client station (Marketing Society, 1982).

It is important to remember, therefore, that not all recall studies are equivalent. Higher levels of listening will be generated where the level of prompting is higher, the reconstruction of the day's listening is thorough and the criterion of 'listening' is loose.

Diaries

The respondent is asked to keep a diary of radio listening for a period of time. Thus a week or more of data can be derived from one interview. Again, there is an immense variety of techniques available. Diaries may be personally placed and collected, or either or both of these operations may be conducted by post. Telephone may be used for recruitment, followed by postal placement and retrieval.

Diaries vary considerably in terms of layout. They may have time scales to be ticked or they may require entries to be made of times for starting and finishing listening sessions. Stations may be printed for the listener to tick or he or she may have to write in the station listened to. In consequence, diary studies, like recall studies, are not equivalent.

Diaries have a major advantage in that they minimise reliance upon memory and help to reduce confusion over station identification. They potentially run the risk that people more interested in radio are more likely to co-operate, although the alternative hypothesis that heavy listeners may be deterred by the onerousness of the task may also apply. It is clearly important to maximise co-operation for all types of listener.

The memory problem is alleviated by diaries in two ways. First, it is clearly possible to record at or near the time of the event, although in practice some diary-keeping in arrears is inevitable. Second, the fact of keeping a diary has the crucial effect of prompting awareness that radio listening is to be remembered. This is a prerequisite for the formation of memories in some circumstances.

General habits

Questions can be asked of respondents about when they usually listen and what they usually listen to. These can be expressed in terms of estimated frequency of listening to different stations at different times. It is not difficult to translate such data into average probabilities of listening at different times.

Major problems are that much radio listening is not based on habit, certainly not to anything like the degree that television is, with its series or serials, nor like much of press readership. The task for the respondent is to summarise a whole range of casual events without being provided with the context or content cues to reconstruct even a single day. Media habit questions are generally difficult for respondents to answer, but they are especially difficult for radio. The analysis above must suggest that there is a risk of underestimating radio listening where casual listening is a high proportion of the whole. For media that are heavily habit-based, the reverse is likely in that in practice people do not quite complete the totality of what they regard as their general habits.

Coincidental interviewing

This involves interviewing people about their radio listening here and now at the moment of interview. It is most appropriate to the measurement of in-home listening levels, but with a great deal of effort, samples of car-drivers (e.g. at traffic lights) have been asked about listening in North American studies. The coincidental approach is prohibitively expensive for any regular measurement – basically, one minute's worth of data is obtained per interview. It has a role, nevertheless, as a yardstick or standard in methodological research because answers are unaffected by memory problems and are potentially verifiable at the moment of the interview.

Recording devices

Radio metering was, in fact, used long before its application to television. The first radio meter patent was filed in 1929 in the USA. The Nielsen Radio Index ran from 1936 to 1964 and combined metered measurement of the tuning of a sample of sets with diaries to measure listeners per set and the demographics of the audience. The demise of the Nielsen service was due in large part to the steady growth in car radios, the explosion in the number of small portables, and the rise in multi-set ownership. While, technologically, some of these problems can be overcome, the funds available would not be sufficient to match the investment in technology needed. It is, in short, no longer cost-effective to use recording devices in this way. There would also be further problems in measuring casual out-of-home listening, which has become increasingly important.

HOW TECHNIQUES COMPARE IN PRACTICE

Research, much of it in North America, has compared the results of using different techniques in an attempt to establish the validity of radio audience estimates. The earliest was a comprehensive study in the USA called the All Radio Methodology Study (ARMS, 1967), carried out in 1965 for the Advertising Research Foundation. This compared five diary and three recall methods against a standard of in-home listening derived from a telephone coincidental survey amongst 28,000 individuals. These were a random selection of people aged 12 and over prelisted from an earlier probability sample from telephone directories. The idea was to eliminate telephone-answering bias. A car-listening standard was derived from a car-usage survey with coincidental interviewing at road intersections and car metering. The findings are shown in Table 4.2.

Table 4.2   Levels of listening: average percentage quarter-hour all-individual audience (Monday to Friday, 7.00 a.m. to 10.00 p.m.)

Standard: coincidental at home + car	13.8
Radio, daily diaries	16.0–16.5
Radio, weekly diaries – telephone/mail-in	15.5
Radio, weekly diaries – personal placement and collection	13.6
Four-media diaries	8.2
Personal DAR radio	12.1
Telephone DAR radio	9.7
Telephone DAR, four-media	8.6

Three key conclusions may be drawn from this study:

- day-after-recall (DAR) techniques produce lower listening levels,
- covering other media at the same time depresses reported radio listening levels,
- weekly radio-only diaries with personal placement and collection gives the nearest result to the standard.

Another North American study for the American Research Bureau/ RKO General Broadcasting (1965), showed broadly similar results from comparing in-home listening from a multi-media diary, a radio-only diary, a telephone interview and a telephone coincidental, although it was the multi-media diary that checked out best with the coincidental standard.

A slightly later North American study reported in 1967 as the 'Polyphase' study (Radio Advertising Representatives), while reinforcing the idea that lower listening levels are obtained by recall than with a diary, also had recall data from people who had refused to take a diary. The latter group showed considerably lower levels of listening. The results suggest that, with low levels of response, co-operation bias tended to inflate reported listening for diaries. The results are shown in Table 4.3.

The North American studies, taken together, indicate that the exact ways in which the techniques are conducted, probably interacting with local conditions, determine the levels of listening reported, and consequently whether the level for any technique is in line with the coincidental standard.

Research in Germany, reported by Franz (1991), provides a special

Table 4.3   Average number of quarter-hours listening per respondent,
Monday to Friday: daily average, 6.00 a.m. to 6.00 p.m., AM
and FM radio.

	Diary co-operators	*Diary non-co-operators*
Chicago		
Recall	11.2	8.8
Diary	13.0	
San Francisco		
Recall	9.2	7.4
Diary	10.8	

case where recall was conducted so thoroughly that it yielded listening levels similar to diaries. Here, respondents reconstructed their previous day in great detail, recalling all activities including radio listening. This 'daily routines' approach was used both with recall and with diaries, both yielding higher listening levels than conventional radio diaries. The listening audiences were compared with coincidental checks at selected points. The coincidental levels were, overall, the highest, with the daily routine methods very close.

The study thus showed that if enough care is taken to reconstruct memory, then recall of listening to radio can match the levels obtained by the diary, which prompts people to take note of their behaviour. That coincidentally checked listening levels were highest of all once again confirms the validity of the higher levels of listening reported by diaries. This research can be related to results from the ARMS study to suggest that there is a general principle within recall that the more intensive the questioning in terms of opportunities to provide reconstruction of activities, the higher the listening levels reported. Thus the 'daily routines' approach would yield higher levels than conventional personal interview aided recall, which in turn in the ARMS study produced higher levels than telephone recall.

From Canada the Bureau of Broadcast Measurement (1973, 1974–5) reported the results of a test comparing the existing two-media diary that combined radio and television with a revised version of this diary and a radio-only diary. Compared with the existing diary the modified two-media diary slightly reduced levels of in-home radio listening, while the radio-only diary increased them. A telephone coincidental check on both radio and television levels revealed that the radio-only diary returners were heavier radio listeners then non-returners, and that the radio-only diary-keepers were recording their levels of listening accurately.

Earlier methodological work had suggested that, for the two-media diary, respondents were likely to be heavier listeners than non-responders, but that they under-reported their listening. The result of the compensating errors gave correct overall levels of listening. The conclusion to be drawn from these studies is that small differences in technique change reported levels of listening. While listening is correctly reported in a diary, lighter listeners are likely to be lost to a diary sample if the response rate is low. Later research that involved intensive interviews for diary-keepers showed that, for the two-media diary, errors for radio greatly outnumbered those for television and resulted in under-reporting.

In the UK the results from a JICRAR survey in 1975 showing that the average weekly hours recorded in a diary was 22.3 were compared with the results of asking the same people for their 'usual' radio listening habits at an earlier stage. Levels of listening were considerably depressed at 13.8 hours (JICRAR, 1975). In 1988 the BBC conducted an experiment in Sheffield on the results of recall versus diaries (Menneer, 1989; Twyman, 1989). For many years the BBC ran a day-after recall measurement system, while the independent stations, carrying advertising and working with an industry committee (JICRAR), used diaries. The diaries yielded substantially higher listening claims. The BBC conducted a formal experiment whereby respondents first gave an aided recall interview and subsequently kept diaries. The experiment also compared two alternative criteria of listening as a basis for completing the quarter-hour diaries: any listening in the quarter-hour versus listening to more than half of the quarter-hour. The results (see Table 4.4) showed that the criteria made little difference, but demonstrated the usual relationships between recall and diaries.

Recent work by the newly formed Radio Joint Audience Research (RAJAR) has shown that there is a positive correlation between claimed usual behaviour and actual listening measured by diaries, but the match is far from perfect. Even some of those claiming never to listen to the radio

Table 4.4 Weekly hours of listening

Quarter-hour criteria	More than half	Any listening in quarter-hour
Recall	13.65	14.70
Diary (post recall)	17.73	18.93
Diary increase	+31%	+29%

record some listening in their diaries. 'Usual listening', like most reported usual behaviour, probably represents a mixture of motivation, intention and attitude.

The evidence reviewed so far shows, in short, that, to varying degrees, reported listening levels are depressed where:

- there is reliance on memory and recall techniques,
- there is competition with other media,
- there is less intensive questioning,
- there is 'usual habits' questioning.

Asking about radio listening in the context of other media (particularly television) depresses the levels of reported listening. This is probably because the nature of television viewing is highly purposive; it involves being in the right place at the right time and abandoning other activities. When radio is considered in this context, listening in parallel with other activities, accidental or imposed by other people, may be ignored. The ARMS study reported above shows that, compared with the standard, the introduction of other media generates considerable under-claiming for either diaries or telephone day-after recall.

At the end of the day one is left asking whether the higher levels of listening generally reported in diaries are in fact 'true' and what they mean in terms of media exposure. The evidence reviewed so far suggests that they can be true in the sense of checking against a coincidentally reported level.

It is worth considering further what 'exposure' means in these terms. The definition of radio listening is highly subjective and in the absence of clear explanation respondents can exclude certain categories. The BBM 1974–5 programme of research included some intensive interviews on a relatively large sample of respondents about their diary keeping. It was found in two sets of these interviews that a major source of error in diary-keeping was uncertainty or ambiguity in recording 'listening' not found in anything like the same degree in television. There was a tendency for some respondents not to report listening if they were doing something else at the time, if they were not paying full attention, or if they did not control the tuning decision.

The subsequent validation check on the BBM diaries showed that the levels of listening from different techniques could in fact be equated with those of different levels of attention as checked in a coincidental interview. The diary level corresponded to hearing radio rather than actively chosen listening. For most purposes this is what the user of the data requires. For the broadcaster, it represents the audience actually listening, intentionally or not. For the advertiser, the source of the audience is unimportant; it is whether they have the opportunity to hear the advertisement that counts.

THE ORGANISATION OF RADIO RESEARCH IN THE UK

As with most media research, techniques for measuring radio audiences are usually employed within continuous or regular research systems. These may be illustrated by the development of radio audience research in the UK. Initially, radio broadcasting was solely within the remit of the BBC until commercial radio, preceded by 'pirate' broadcasting, began. The BBC was, and still is, funded from the licence fee and cannot sell advertising. As a public-service broadcaster, it has operated a range of stations, providing news, information, general entertainment, light entertainment, classical music and popular music. Before the general availability of television, these services occupied much the same role as television does today, and a research system was set up to meet the needs of such a role, namely daily reporting on a programme-by-programme basis. Since the advent of universal television, however, radio has become more specialised in the areas of music, news and information, although BBC Radio 4 has continued the tradition of diversity of programme content. Audience research needs had to change in parallel.

The research system initially devised by the BBC was a Daily Survey with a sample of massive proportions and involved interviewing up to 3,000 people every day of the year. This was subsequently reduced to 1,000 in-home individual interviews until the system was abandoned in 1992. The technique used was day-after recall, with radio followed by television and general broadcasting questions.

The survey originally provided daily audience data. Later, with the reduced sample, programme data were produced monthly, and overall listening levels were published only weekly. For the main BBC stations, being national, very large samples were available when analysed over longer periods. For the growing number of BBC local stations, however, even a large national survey was not adequate, so supplementary surveys were conducted for local stations.

The final form of the Daily Survey was 1,000 individual in-home interviews per day, including boosted samples for Wales and Northern Ireland. For local stations not adequately covered by the Daily Survey, there were 'sweeps' in spring and autumn. These comprised 1,500 individual interviews per local station. These could be conducted in the street and were spread over four weeks with 500 interviews on weekdays combined, and 500 each on Saturdays and Sundays.

The BBC local samples reflected the changing requirements away from individual programme audiences to 'typical' audiences for consistently formated programming, often with high music, news and information content. The requirements of commercial radio, when it eventually came, were similar. Commercial radio appeared relatively late in the UK in the form of Independent Local Radio (ILR), starting in 1973. The primary requirement was to provide services centred on, and identified with, specific localities and financed by the sale of advertising. The franchises for stations were originally awarded by the Independent Broadcasting Authority (IBA), which also awarded the Independent Television franchises. This body has now been split up, and radio comes under the Radio Authority, which awards licences and issues binding codes of practice on programming, advertising, sponsorship and engineering. The IBA formerly had responsibility for building and maintaining transmitters, but this function has now been privatised and is operated by National Trans Com (NTC). Stations can, however, utilise other sources for transmitters.

Independent *national* radio (INR) stations have now begun under the Radio Authority. The first such station was Classic FM, which opened in 1992; this was followed by Virgin Radio, which began broadcasting in 1993, although only on medium wave, which is restricted to mono broadcasting.

Initially the requirements for ILR audience research were based on measuring a typical audience on a periodic basis. The frequency of measurement was limited by the regionality of the medium. A large number of relatively small local stations each require a separate sample of adequate size (the general rule is currently a minimum of 500 respondents). This greatly magnifies the cost of research relative to a national medium. Similar problems, of course, arise for other regional media, for example local press (see Chapter 5).

ILR originally worked with an industry body – the Joint Industry Committee for Radio Audience Research (JICRAR) – which determined research and reporting standards. JICRAR was comprised of representatives of independent radio companies, advertising agencies, media independents and advertisers each organised through their respective industry bodies. The research specification was based on samples of diary-keepers with a minimum sample size of 500 per station, initially spread over four weeks.

The survey used to be carried out annually, but in 1987 it went over to continuous fieldwork throughout the year. The problem with this was that the smaller stations had to wait for a year before the accumulated sample size was large enough to make sensible estimates. So in 1989 the system was changed again so that there were four quarterly 'sweeps' of eight weeks each. However, since not every station wanted four lots of research a year, one sweep or 'wave' was to be the universal quarter (undertaken in the spring) in which all members were expected to participate. The other quarters were to be optional, although for the winter quarter the larger stations were expected to take part. The eight-week sweeps, however, it was felt by air-time buyers, were open to abuse since the big stations could still make uncharacteristic promotional efforts during the crucial eight weeks to boost their figures. So, the waves were extended to 12 weeks, making 48 weeks of research in all, but compared with the earlier continuous surveys, the whole thing had to be set up four times a year, with four sets of independent samples and so on. This made it an expensive operation and there were ongoing debates about the rules of enforced participation.

There are arguments for and against spreading research over a longer period versus restricting it to a short typical period. Spreading research means that it is not at the mercy of atypical events, but assumes unchanging programme schedules which achieve stable audiences. Concentrating research can avoid the problem of programme schedules changing in the middle of a research period and this strategy is therefore more interpretable in programming terms.

Discussions between the BBC, the ILR companies and JICRAR, bearing in mind the likely requirements of INR, have eventually resulted in a new joint audience research contract and a new joint industry body called RAJAR (Radio Joint Audience Research). The RAJAR specification was drawn up to meet the requirements on all sides, put out to tender, and research started in October 1992. Meeting so many requirements around ILR stations, BBC local stations and a variety of national stations resulted in a necessarily complex research specification, probably the most complex media research system ever (Gane, 1992).

The new radio audience measurement system again uses a one-week diary, but unlike the earlier JICRAR system, sampling is now on a household basis, and diaries are placed with all members of the household through a responsible contact. This technique is known as 'flooding' in Canada, where it is believed to lead to a higher response rate; it is also believed to reach more of the 'hard to contact' listeners. The correlation between the listening behaviour of members of the same household, however, reduced the effective sample size. This finding is reflected in the new system in a minimum reporting sample size of 650 corresponding to the previous minimum of 500 'independent' respondents required by JICRAR.

The one-week self-completion diary incorporates a time grid with named stations as column headings. It covers every day of the week, every week of the year. A national sample of 14,500 adults aged 15 and over, and 2,400 children aged 4–14, is taken every quarter, with samples spread uniformly over the weeks. Wales is disproportionately sampled up to 1,000, and Northern Ireland up to 650. Regional samples are created by boosting in local areas for the second and fourth quarter in each year.

A particularly complex feature of this research is the structure of local and national samples. The overlaying of independent local station areas on BBC local station areas creates over 300 geographical segments. The national sample is distributed across these according to population. For local station areas, the samples sizes required in each segment is calculated and the number needed to boost the national sample allocation to that level is determined. Local samples are then built up by starting with the needs of the smallest station in each segment, that is, the one that requires the maximum boost. Each segment needs a different diary design listing the appropriate stations. All receivable ILR and BBC local stations for an area are included as named columns in the diary. The addition of new national stations – Atlantic 252, Classic FM and Virgin Radio – further increases the number of named stations which is as high as 23 in some cases. There is some possibility that the limits of what is feasible without confusion have been reached or perhaps even exceeded. The design of diaries for increasing numbers of stations is a task for the future.

An associated problem is that of station identification. In almost all in-depth methodological research, respondents' problems with station names and identities is evident. Stations need to maintain a very clear, consistent, noticeable and frequent branding. Creative solutions will be needed both for correct station identification and the ever-growing number of stations that pose problems for research.

A feature of the new system is that the selection of samples, the printing of diaries, the generation of interviewers' assignments are all handled by computer. National data are processed every month with quarterly reporting.

EXTENDED REACH AND ADVERTISING SCHEDULE ANALYSIS

The one-week diary limits the measurement of station reach to seven days. In the UK, station reach over longer periods has been estimated by the use of a model using an exponential function. The parameters of this model have been determined by occasional four-week diary studies. A potential disadvantage of the use of such diaries is diminishing response rates that can change the nature of the sample over time, and possibly less thorough diary completion over time. Every effort needs to be made to minimise these effects.

The limit to advertising schedule coverage is clearly set by station reach. In the UK ready-reckoners have been developed for calculating net cover for advertising schedules, for example the RASCAL formula developed by Gullen (1982). The schedule net cover in per cent (*C*) is calculated from gross rating points (*G*) and station reach over the period of the campaign (*R*) by taking:

$$C = \frac{G \times R}{G + R} - 2$$

Capital Radio modified this by having a constant of +1 instead of − 2. Generally, however, these formulae have predicted coverage to within a few points. They are likely to be specific to broadcasting context, but illustrate a potential approach to this issue.

RADIO AUDIENCE APPRECIATION

There is a growing interest among broadcasters, and to some extent among advertisers, in appreciation of programmes, although primarily so far for television. (The BBC has had a radio listening panel since 1941, but it covers only the BBC's networked stations.) The relevance to broadcasters is obvious for programme planning and scheduling. Advertisers' interest is based on the belief that favourable programme attitudes may beneficially affect advertising reception. Relationships between radio-ratings appreciation and attention are discussed in de Haas (1991).

CONCLUSION

The nature of the medium and its great strength of being receivable in a wide variety of contexts makes it difficult to research. It is likely that increasing numbers of stations, together with further extensions to a variety of reception modes, will increase problems with both recall and diaries. It is possible that new techniques will need to be developed to deal with these circumstances. One possibility is a reasonably in-depth interview to establish which stations are listened to, followed by a specially created diary using stick-in station headings. Such a diary is already being tried experimentally in the USA. Electronic methods of recording are difficult because of the uncontrolled range of reception sources to which a respondent is exposed. The only electronic solution that would not be unfavourable to radio is the 'wristwatch meter' that recognises signals. This, according to Weinblatt and Douglas (1992), is technologically possible.

REFERENCES

American Research Bureau/RKO General Broadcasting (1965) *The Individual Diary Method of Radio Audience Measurement*, New York, ARB.

ARMS (1967) *All Radio Methodology Study*, New York, Audits and Surveys Inc.

Bureau of Broadcast Measurement (1973) *Tests of Revised and Single Media Diaries*. Toronto, BBM.

Bureau of Broadcast Measurement (1974–5) *Research Programme 1974–5*, Toronto, BBM.

Day, C., Wilkins, C., Twyman, T. and Woodham, G. (1984) 'The Psychology of Radio Listening', in *Proceedings of the 37th ESOMAR Congress*, Rome, September; Amsterdam, European Society for Opinion and Marketing Research.

De Haas, W. (1991), 'Attention for and Appreciation of Radio Programmes: Quantitative Aspects of Media Behaviour', in *The Expansion of the Broadcast Media: Does Research Meet the Challenges?*, ESOMAR Seminar, Madrid, January; Amsterdam, ESOMAR.

Franz, G. (1991) 'Methods of Radio Audience Measurement Comparing Interview and Diary Techniques', in *The Expansion of the Broadcast Media: Does Research Meet the Challenges?*, ESOMAR Seminar, Madrid, January; Amsterdam, ESOMAR.

Gane, R. (1992) 'RAJAR: The UK's New Radio Audience Research Service', *ADMAP*, November.

Gullen, P. (1982) 'The Rascal that Helped Capital', *Media World*, December.

JICRAR (1975) *London Survey*, May, London, Association of Independent Radio Companies.

Marketing Society, Ireland (1982) *Report by Professional Purposes Sub-Committee*, September, Dublin.

Menneer, P. (1989) 'Towards a Radio BARB: Some Issues of Measurement', *ADMAP*, February.

Radio Advertising Representatives (1967) *Polyphase Radio Listening and the Problems of its Measurement*, New York, RAR.

Twyman, T. (1989) 'Measuring the Total Radio Audience: A Rejoinder to Peter Menneer', London, *ADMAP*, March.

Weinblatt, L. and Douglas, S. (1992) 'A Presentation of the TV, Radio and Print Applications of the First Intermedia Personal Meter: A Review of its Development Strengths and Weaknesses', in *First ARF/ESOMAR Worldwide Broadcast Audience Research Symposium*, Toronto, June; Amsterdam, ESOMAR/New York, ARF.

FURTHER READING

Teer, F. (1986) 'Radio, Outdoor and Cinema Research', in R. Worcester and J. Downham (eds) *Consumer Market Research Handbook*, Amsterdam, ESOMAR, Ch. 26.

Bloom, D. (1984) 'Radio: Problems in Measuring the Invisible Medium', *Proceedings of the 27th Annual Conference*, Market Research Society, London.

Chapter 5

Estimating newspaper and magazine readership

Michael Brown

INTRODUCTION

To many non-specialists, the estimation of the size of mass media audiences must seem a way of life at best arcane and, at worst, of very dubious relevance to the 'real' world. In none of the areas covered in these chapters is such an image likely to hold more true than in the case of readership research – the measurement of newspapers' and magazines' audiences. The budgets for such research run to millions of ECUs annually; there have been six international symposia on the subject and many specialised seminars; a myriad of conference and journal papers have been written; and yet, after all this activity, a vociferous stable of readership research experts and consultants around the world continues to debate the merits and demerits of alternative technical approaches and the relative validity of their respective findings. How, the outsider may reasonably ask, is it possible to justify the attempt to crowd so many angels onto one, modest-sized pin?

As in many other areas of audience measurement, the commercial importance of readership research stems from the fact that newspapers and magazines carry advertising and are dependent on this revenue source – heavily dependent, in the case of a 'popular' national newspaper, which might rely on advertisement space sales for 70 per cent of its revenue and totally so in the case of a suburban 'freesheet'.

Considering the portion of total advertising expenditure devoted to print media, the division of this spend *between* the many different titles available as potential advertising vehicles is closely related to the size and nature of the audiences they offer, considered in conjunction, of course, with their advertising rates. Further, on the basis of mutual agreement between the buyer and the seller of advertising space in print media, readership estimates have come to be the 'currency' in which the medium is traded, so that there is considerable pressure to fund the regular collection of detailed and defensible readership data.

At the same time, it is not to be overlooked that many publications offer examples of joint supply; they operate in *two* markets – the market for advertising opportunities, just discussed, and the market for copies. Thus readership data are also of relevance to editorial and circulation departments, as evidence of the success (or otherwise) of attracting the size and profile of audience aimed for via a particular policy on editorial contents and their treatment. However, in practice, the research results find far less application in these areas than in relation to ad sales.

MEASURING READERSHIP

Viewed as behaviour, there are a number of difficulties in trying to pin down what the activity of 'reading' encompasses. First, it covers a wide spectrum, from the cursory glance to thorough perusal of a publication, occupying some considerable time period. Then again, 'I read the *Ambridge Weekly Echo*' will usually mean, in practice, 'I regularly read (if I have time) those sections and items which most interest me personally, I glance at others and I skip some pages completely'. Lastly, we must carefully distinguish between 'eyes-open-in-front-of-the-page', as offering an opportunity for perception – but no more than an opportunity – and the actual transfer of content from that page to a reader's mind and memory.

In attempting to measure the size of print media audiences, much readership research takes, as its focus of measurement, an *issue* of a newspaper or magazine, rather than an editorial section or a page or an advertisement. When the findings speak of 'issue readership', they do not necessarily imply thorough reading; if any threshold of intensity of contact is set, it is most likely to be a relatively low one. Furthermore, 'readership research', as usually understood, is not concerned with communication effects or effectiveness, whether in relation to editorial contents or advertisements. It is on these conventions that this chapter is based (although we shall touch on within-the-issue readership and contact with ads).

There are then three main problems to be faced in any measurement of print media audiences.

First, the estimates obtained are heavily dependent on the particular operational definition of what is to count as 'reading' that is adopted; the more 'tightly' is reading defined, the smaller will be the resultant audience estimate.

Second, many reading events are not particularly memorable, particularly if they relate to publications seen infrequently, irregularly or happenstantially; readers can well report what they perceive as their habitual or usual behaviour – but researchers are often concerned with total reading, exceptions and all.

Third, it is extremely difficult – if not impossible – to establish an external, 'yardstick' measurement of readership, against which the validity of alternative measures may be evaluated. Estimates of purchases based on consumer panels may be checked against actual sales; television and radio audience estimates can be compared with 'coincidental' measurements, taken at or very close to the time viewing or listening occurs; but no such yardsticks are readily available for checking readership.

DATA COLLECTION METHODS FOR READERSHIP RESEARCH

The main methods of data collection between which the researcher will need to choose include face-to-face interviews, telephone research, questionnaires despatched and/or returned by post and electronic data-collection.

Despite the relatively high unit cost and the increasing difficulty, in many countries, of maintaining response rates (the ratio, that is, of achieved interviews to the number of people preselected for interview, using probability sampling), personal contact remains in very wide use for readership measurement. There are two main reasons. The first is the necessity to maintain rapport during a lengthy interview, which can well run to three-quarters of an hour or more as a survey average, this timing being dictated not only by the length of the media list to be covered but also by the host of subsidiary, non-readership questions that will often be asked.

The second consideration strongly favouring face-to-face interviewing is the difficulty that the reader may have in correctly identifying, in their own mind, *which* publication they are being asked about, particularly in cases where they see some particular newspaper or magazine only irregularly or where there exist closely similar-sounding titles. (The story is oft repeated of the dear lady who, many years ago, wrote to Odhams Press, as it then was, congratulating the editor on the quality of his magazine, but wondering why he chose to title it, some weeks, *Woman* but, on other occasions, *Woman's Own*). The best way, it is felt, to minimise this difficulty – which certainly exists – is to prompt people visually; and this is difficult to achieve other than by an interviewer carrying the necessary field materials around with her.

Given the rising costs of personal interviewing and the increasing difficulties of effecting contact with an adequately representative sample (in deprived inner-city areas, for example, or amongst blocks of flats guarded by entryphones), telephone interviewing has become the preferred – and effective – alternative in many areas of marketing research. For readership measurement, it is in wide use in America in relation to newspapers, but not for magazine surveys; in Europe, telephone interviewing has become strongly associated with one particular measurement approach – 'First Reading Yesterday' – to which we return later in this chapter. There are, however, some limitations: maintaining rapport and co-operation throughout a lengthy and, unavoidably, somewhat repetitive interview may not be easy by telephone; and the sole prompts to aid correct identification of newspapers and magazines must be their titles.

Readership surveys conducted by post are relatively commonplace, but usually in relation to a small, specialised audience, widely dispersed geographically, which it would be extremely expensive to sample by any other means. The main limitations lie in the necessary use of a self-completion questionnaire, the relatively low response rate to be expected (even if some form of incentive is employed) and consequent doubts as to the representativeness of the achieved sample.

Self-completion methods can and do have a considerable place in readership research, particularly when the media audience data are being collected within the context of some much larger questionnaire, for which the method is well-suited; but there are two quite serious limitations. Completely open-ended questions – 'What do you read?' – are rare in this field and can be shown generally to lead to considerable underclaiming; nearly always, the answers will be prompted by the names of the publications to be covered, by illustrations of their logos or 'mastheads', by examples of their covers or by complete issues. But under self-completion conditions, there can be no effective control over the reader's use of the prompts that are provided; in particular, there can be no guarantee that each one is given equal and balanced attention, so that biases do not arise which favour the more salient and well-known titles.

A second self-completion limitation lies in order effects. Whilst readership research can be (and sometimes is) conducted in relation to a very small number of titles – amongst a group of non-consumer magazines appealing to a highly specialised audience, for example – the more common situation will be for the 'media list' to run to tens or even hundreds of publications. Under such conditions, it will be commonplace for the data collected to display 'order effects': the readership claims made will depend, numerically, on the ordinal position of the title concerned within the questionnaire and/or on which specific publications have preceded it. This problem is conventionally tackled by administering a readership questionnaire in a number of different, balanced orders, amongst different sub-samples. However, even if several such different versions of a self-completion questionnaire are prepared, there can again be no guarantee that they will actually be read and completed in the orders in which they are printed.

Under this heading we should also note the possibility of printing some form of readership questionnaire actually in the pages of a newspaper or magazine, or of enclosing one with a particular issue or issues. The considerations attaching to self-completion and to response rate apply here too, but, additionally, there is the problem that such a questionnaire can only be completed, generally speaking, by the one person who 'owns' the copy concerned; little or no data will be provided about readers to whom copies are passed on, who may comprise a sizeable proportion of the total audience. Thus, whilst such 'in-page' questionnaires, as they are called, probably offer a publisher the very cheapest means of collecting at least some information about his audience, they are not to be recommended.

The fourth possibility as regards readership data capture is to employ electronic means (over and above the possibility of providing personal interviewers with portable computers, in place of pencil-and-paper questionnaires): a questionnaire may be displayed on a household's normal television screen, or on a VDU attached to a specially installed terminal; and that questionnaire may be transmitted to the household from the researcher either as part of a television signal – on-air or cabled – or via a pair of telephone lines.

In such circumstances, visual prompts may be fully used while the questionnaire and the order in which it is administered remain as much under the researcher's control as in the face-to-face interview situation. The data are instantly available for editing and analysis the moment they are keyed in by a respondent, using either a standard computer keyboard or a keypad resembling a TV set's remote control. However, per household, the costs of the equipment, of installation and of maintenance of the system are relatively high, so that such research is likely to be based on a relatively small sample of people, repetitively questioned over some continuous period.

Whatever the method of data collection employed, the researcher will also need to decide whether the study is to be *ad hoc* or repeated at regular intervals or whether continuous measurement should be employed and, in either of the latter two cases, whether to use independent samples or a panel.

A readership survey conducted regularly with, say, the interviewing occupying the same few weeks each year or two years is organisationally simple and offers apparent comparability of results; but it can take no account of any seasonal patterns which may exist and, should the fixed fieldwork period coincide, unfortunately, with abnormal conditions in the marketplace – an international catastrophe, pushing up newspaper sales, perhaps, or a strike amongst distribution staff – then the data may rapidly become very *a*typical. Conducting readership fieldwork continuously, throughout the year, with reports published, say, six-monthly, based on a rolling year's sample overcomes these problems, to a degree – but at the price that it naturally takes longer to accumulate a given size of sample, so that the results are relatively less up-to-the-minute, when published; the mid-point of the interviewing period is some considerable period earlier than the data release date.

To research not only continuously, but also amongst a constant sample or panel represents a more major decision. If it is readership trends that are of most interest, or period-on-period changes, then a panel may offer advantages in terms of statistical cost-efficiency; but since the research cost per panel member may be considerably higher than it would be per respondent in an *ad hoc* readership survey, panel sizes tend to be modest, with consequences for the precision of point-in-times estimates of absolute readership levels, as contrasted with changes. Unfortunately, the arguments for and against a readership panel *per se* often become clouded by the advantages and limitations of whatever method is selected for collecting the data from panel members, which may often be some form of diary. To this we return later.

MEASURING AVERAGE ISSUE READERSHIP: THE ALTERNATIVES

The audience size of a newspaper or magazine is usually measured in terms of *average issue* readership – the number of different people, that is to say, who read a single issue, averaged across issues. It is possible to ask people whether they recognise a particular issue of some newspaper or magazine as one they have seen before; or to rely on their recall of a previous reading event; or to have them keep a concurrent record, at or near the time of reading. Under the 'recall' option, we can question people about reading that may have taken place some time in the past, or only very recently. That makes four basic alternatives.

Through-the-Book

The first of these is the oldest, is American in origin but, despite the vehemence of the arguments of its protagonists, is only in limited current use, worldwide. It is called the 'Through-the-Book' (TTB) technique. It has an interesting history, dating from 1936 when the magazine *Life* discovered that several of its issues were selling out almost as fast as they reached the newsstands. People who wanted to read them were therefore forced to obtain them from purchasers. It followed that circulation figures *per se* could not reflect the total audience of *Life* which represented, it was hoped, a significant bonus for advertisers.

The team assembled to solve the problem of measuring *Life*'s total audience did so by sampling the population, showing people a particular issue, taking them through it page by page and asking if they had read key articles.

In these early days of the TTB method, it was recognised that people might make false claims, confusing an issue shown them but previously unseen with another, similar one they *had* read. A 'confusion control' correction was therefore introduced: pre-publication issues were shown to a sample of people and the proportion claiming to have read them (which was impossible) was deducted from the TTB scores for 'live' issues.

Confusion control thus demanded a costly research technique with difficult logistics, whilst the corrections seldom amounted to more than 1 per cent or 2 per cent of the TTB levels. It has been completely succeeded by the 'editorial interest' variant of TTB, which is still with us today, having been first proposed in 1940 by Louise McCarthy, a researcher at *Life*. Here, people are taken through a specific issue as before, and asked 'Does this look interesting?' in relation to each of a number of key items. This completed, the interviewer asks, almost as a throwaway, 'Just for the record, are you sure you have (haven't) seen this issue before, or aren't you certain about it?' The levels of 'Yes, sure' replies obtained when this approach was first introduced were very close to the original TTB claims, after confusion-control correction.

The TTB method has undergone two other important changes since its inception, which it is important to understand.

In the early days, TTB surveys related to a single magazine, or at most a few, so that it was quite practicable for an interviewer to carry round full, complete copies of the issues to be used in the test. However, as demands from publishers and advertisers grew, so the researchers' media lists lengthened and the interviewer's armful of magazines grew first to a trunkful, then to a truckful. The only remedy was a move to 'stripped-down' or skeletonised issues, containing but a proportion of the original full complement of pages but hopefully enough cues to lead to correct identification of an issue as 'seen before' or 'not seen'. (Full-page ads are, in any case, generally excluded, since they recur over issues and in different publications, potentially blurring the correct recognition of specific copies.)

The other change is that, at the outset of the method's use, no critical questions were put before the test issues were shown and everyone was asked about them. Nowadays, this is not so: with a long list of magazines to handle, a 'filter' or 'hurdle' question heads the interview: presented, typically, with reproductions of the publications' logos on small, separate cards, a respondent is asked to sort them into groups comprising the ones she has and has not read at all within, say, the past year. Only for the titles thus 'screened in' are the stripped-down issues then actually shown.

Recent Reading

The second method for estimating average issue readership is British. It is more recent than TTB, having first seen the light of day in the 1950s and predominates (with modifications) in present-day use. It is called the Recent Reading (RR) technique or, sometimes still, the IPA method, from its first application in the surveys then sponsored by the Institute of Practitioners in Advertising (or 'Incorporated Practitioners', at the outset, if we wish to be fully accurate).

The key differences between TTB and RR are that the latter method relies on the recall of having read any issue of a particular publication, rather than on the recognition of a specific issue as previously seen.

In the Recent Reading methodology, people are prompted on each of a number of newspapers and magazines, either in terms of just their titles or, more usually, by being shown their logos – but other prompts may also be employed, such as sets of typical covers. For each publication, a key question or series of questions then establishes when a person claims to have most recently read or looked at *any* issue of that newspaper or magazine. It does not matter whether the issue was a current one or not; the reading can have taken place anywhere and the issue seen may or may not have been the personal property of the reader. Critically, the RR model then goes on to argue that an unbiased estimate of the number of people seeing the average issue is provided by the number reading any issue within a period of time immediately preceding the day of interview and equal in length to the interval between the appearance of successive issues

– seven days, for example, in the case of a Sunday newspaper or weekly magazine. This interval is usually referred to as the 'issue period'.

The Recent Reading technique presents two problems which must be mentioned immediately, although a fuller, comparative assessment of all the main methods is held over until later in this chapter.

First, the accuracy of the method depends critically on readers being able to report precisely when they last saw an issue of a particular publication; such accuracy is not easy to achieve, particularly when contact with a given newspaper or magazine is irregular or infrequent – and the longer ago the reading event was, the worse the problem becomes.

Second, there is, unfortunately, an inbuilt bias in the method (which was not immediately recognised on its introduction). A person may well read and reread a single issue over an interval longer than the issue period – for example, a television programme magazine published on the Thursday of the week preceding the one it covers has a natural 'life' of ten days or so; and a person may look at two or more different issues of the same publication within one issue period. In the first case, the Recent Reading approach will, unavoidably, over-estimate average issue readership; in the latter circumstances, there will be under-estimation. Technically, these phenomena are referred to as 'replicated readership' and 'parallel readership', respectively; collectively, in the Recent Reading context, they comprise 'model bias'.

First Reading Yesterday

The third basic method – 'First Reading Yesterday' (FRY) – aims to cure both these problems at one blow. Its questioning sequence concentrates on the newspapers and magazines a respondent saw 'yesterday' – the day before the interview – and, for each publication encountered on that day, the FRY method establishes whether the issue that was seen was read yesterday *for the first time*. It is then argued that the number of 'first time readers yesterday', multiplied by the number of days in the issue period provides an estimate of average issue readership (although the calculation method employed in practice differs somewhat from this.)

Using FRY, the strain on memory is thus minimised and recall accuracy maximised, by going no further back in time than 'yesterday', whilst the possibilities of both over- and under-counting are eliminated since, however many times a publication is picked up and over however long a period it is read, for one reader and one issue, there can be only one first reading occasion.

Two comments on the FRY concept are desirable. There is nothing

.

magic about the choice of a single day – 'yesterday' – as the period within which first reading is to be estimated; for example, we could count the number of 'first readers' of a monthly magazine within a week and then multiply the result by four to obtain our AIR estimate. But research judgement suggests that the task of labelling a reading event as 'first' or 'not first', for the copy concerned, becomes increasingly difficult, the further back in time is the event in question.

In those countries where it is now established – principally the Netherlands, where it was launched, and Denmark – the use of FRY has become linked to Computer Assisted Telephone Interviewing (CATI) as the data collection method; consequently, any discussion of the technique's advantages and limitations becomes blurred by the strengths and weaknesses of conducting readership research by telephone. However, there is absolutely no reason at all why the First Reading Yesterday questioning sequence should not be applied in a face-to-face interview or, in principle, in a self-completion questionnaire.

The readership diary

The fourth and last main technique alternative to be briefly described is the readership diary. The principle is a simple one: a representative sample is drawn and each individual in it requested to maintain a record, day-by-day, of what publications they see. The record-keeping period, for any one person, will be at least a week or two and can be much longer – three months, say, or even a year or more.

The format of readership diaries can vary very widely, as can the exact nature of the diary-keeping task. The list of newspapers and magazines on which data are sought can be printed on each diary page; or a look-up directory of publications can be provided to the diary-keeper, with a code beside each title. This code has to be copied into the appropriate space when a reading event takes place. Time periods – days or day-parts, usually – may be pre-printed in the diary, or the respondent called on to record when reading took place, as well as what was read. Again, much or little subsidiary information on each reading event may be called for, which could include the date or serial number of the issue read; whether it was a 'first reading' occasion or not; the source of the copy; or where reading took place.

Just as readership diary layouts and recording tasks vary, so do the methods subsequently used to estimate average issue readership from the data collected. Either Recent Reading or First Reading Yesterday logic may be applied (given, in the latter case, that the diary records capture the issue seen, not just the publication's title); alternatively, measurements of people's regularity of reading may be harnessed, as discussed later in this chapter.

Whilst the readership-diary approach may, at first sight, appear radically different from each of the three others already outlined, it only really possesses two distinguishing features which are of particular importance.

First, the readership diary provides a longitudinal record of a person's reading, over some continuous period of time: regularity and frequency of contact with a given newspaper or magazine may be directly observed in diary data, whilst these variables can only be estimated with limited accuracy from a reader's recall-based replies to a questionnaire administered at a single point in time.

Second, in theory at least, a diary captures reading events at or close to the time that they occur, which will be less true for any recall- or recognition-based readership measurement technique.

Finally here, remember that a diary does not have to comprise a conventional, printed document: a diary page, as already mentioned, could be presented on a VDU screen, in a reader's own home, at a time each day chosen by them and filled in, not with a pencil, but with a light pen, or by clicking a mouse or by entering answers on a computer keyboard.

Comparative advantages and limitations

As noted at the outset of this chapter, it is extraordinarily difficult conclusively to demonstrate the absolute validity of any given readership measurement method. At the same time, however, the research results provide the 'currency' in which newspapers' and magazines' advertisement space is traded. Two consequences follow. In comparing techniques, the best that can usually be hoped for is to strike a judgemental balance between two sets of advantages and disadvantages. Second, in the absence of external validation, probably the most important aim in the design of any particular survey is to minimise relative bias, so as relatively to disadvantage neither individual titles nor groups of publications – newspapers versus magazines, say, or weekly publications versus those published monthly.

Turning, now, to the main techniques described earlier, Through-the-Book, as originally conceived, was an excellent and thorough methodology. It has indubitably been weakened by the introduction of an initial filter question (so that many publications may be accommodated in the one survey, but with detailed questioning applied only to a few) and by the necessary use of stripped-down issues. The evidence suggests that the latter fact may not have a disastrous effect on accurate categorisation of specific issues as 'seen before' or 'not seen', but TTB's filter question provides a specific example of a general evil.

However, the real limitation on TTB accuracy lies elsewhere. The issues shown to respondents are of a particular age; current practice is to use weekly magazines' issues published five or six weeks before the date of interview and 10- or 12-week-old ones for monthly publications. In both instances, the issues are too 'young': at these intervals after publication date, the issues are still collecting new, first-time readers. But to increase test issue age will also increase the proportions of contacts with the issues, early after publication, which would be forgotten by the time of the interview. No fully satisfactory solution to this problem exists, particularly for monthly magazines.

The use of the Recent Reading approach avoids this problem of test issue age and of the long period over which an issue's audience climbs to its final level, since the questioning is in terms of 'any issue'; but there are other worms in its can.

Reference has already been made to the fact that the basic assumption of the method is flawed: the number of people seeing any issue in a certain period is not an unbiased estimate of the number having contact with the average issue. Because 'replicated' and 'parallel' reading can and do occur and because their biasing effects on average issue readership estimates are of opposite directions but, generally speaking, not equal, 'model bias' remains an ineradicable feature of the method, with unequal impact on different publications.

Further, RR estimates critically depend on readers being able to state, with precision, when they last read or looked at any issue of a publication. There is quite strong evidence that 'telescoping' may occur, sometimes if not always; that is to say, relatively long-ago reading events are perceived as having occurred closer to the date of interview than was actually the case. This problem, again, will not have an equal or proportional effect on the estimates for different publications; and again it proffers relatively greater problems for measuring publications appearing monthly or at longer intervals.

Using the First Reading Yesterday approach should eliminate, in principle, most of the problems arising from 'telescoping' (because the recall period is so short) and all of 'model bias' (since first reading comprises a unique event in relation to one person and a particular issue). In assessing this technique, any limitations arising from the use of telephone interviewing should be set aside, since this mode of data collection is not essential. There are, however, other problems.

'First reading' will not be as clear-cut an event for the respondent as it is for the researcher. It is quite a subtle concept and any erroneous categorisation of reading events as between 'first' and 'not first' may have a critical effect on the readership estimates.

Second, the sheer number of reading events taking place 'yesterday', across the FRY survey's sample, will be small; the distribution of reading occasions will be particularly 'thin' for publications published at relatively long intervals and for those with relatively small circulations. Consequently, to give adequate precision, either data must be accumulated over some very considerable period or probabilities must be estimated by aggregating 'similar' titles within a publication group, which can only have the effect of erroneously smoothing-out any real differences.

Third, the estimation of average issue readership on the basis of a period shorter than the issue interval can introduce statistical problems and widen the error margins of the final estimates.

Coming last to the readership diary, no problems of recall *should* occur – and 'first reading' may be directly observed (so long as the diary record includes identification of which issues were read, and not just which newspapers and magazines). But with a self-completion diary, there is no spur to thoroughness and to equal treatment of all titles, other than the panellist's own motivation. Whatever prompt list of publications is provided may or may not be fully used; and without doubt, the diary will not, in all instances, be completed concurrently with the reading events it is to record. Consequently, there may be omissions of irregular, more casual contacts with relatively ill-known titles – and out-of-home reading may not be as fully captured as are in-home events. Both of these effects may work differentially to the greater disadvantage of some titles than others.

MEASURING READING FREQUENCY

When the concept of measuring the total audience or readership of a magazine or newspaper was first conceived, it was also tacitly assumed that 'a reader was a reader was a reader' and that, in respect of any particular publication, a specific person is either 'in' or 'out of' its audience.

A moment's thought will show that neither is this how you (or I) conduct our contact with the press, nor, therefore, does it offer an adequate model of the real world. I *always* consume the *Daily Telegram* over breakfast – except that, last Tuesday, snow stopped my newsagent getting his copies – and by the time I reached the station they'd sold out. As far as 'never' is concerned, I *never* give a thought to *Woman's Life* except that, last July, I was delivering some plum jam to Aunt Agatha's for her birthday and she had a copy on the breakfast room table.

Thus, quite early in readership research history, it became obvious that it was insufficient merely to categorise a person as a 'reader' or a 'non-reader' – it was necessary also to estimate their regularity or frequency of reading. Indeed, it is hardly to exaggerate to say that, as the prime objective of any readership survey, the measurement of average issue readership has been replaced by the estimation of the *probability* of contact with the average issue; it is in this form that the data are very largely now applied.

Information on reading frequency is of considerable importance in three main ways. First, an advertiser will (generally speaking) be more often concerned with placing a series of ads in a publication than a single one. Over the period of his campaign, two figures will be of particular interest to him: how many different people will have any chance of contact with his advertising – 'coverage' – and how often a person will have an opportunity of seeing an ad – 'frequency'. The balance between these two figures is entirely determined by the regularity with which people see the title concerned: the larger the proportion of regular readers amongst its total audience, the lower the coverage, but the higher the frequency – and *vice versa*.

Second, regularity is highly correlated with other, material features of the audience. For example, people who purchase or subscribe to their own copy of a newspaper or magazine will usually be more regular readers than those to whom copies are passed on – and readers in the former group will also be prone to read the issues they see relatively more thoroughly and intensively.

Third, it *may* be possible actually to estimate average issue audience size on the basis of people's claims about their frequency of reading.

As with readership itself, obtaining unbiased estimates of reading frequency is no easy task. We may distinguish four main, alternative approaches: to work with claims, from the same group of people, about their readership of just two different issues of a publication; directly to observe behaviour over several issues; to ask a sample of respondents questions about their *claimed* regularity of reading and to take their answers at face value; or to pose such questions, but then employ some indirect method of turning the answers into probability-of-reading estimates.

The use of just two issues is characteristic of current applications of the Through-the-Book technique. Here, respondents are recontacted at a second interview and questioned on their readership of different issues of the same magazines as they were first shown. From their answers, it is possible to calculate audience 'turnover' – the proportions of the readership of issue one who did and did not read issue two. In itself, this information does not comprise an estimate of reading frequency; however, given knowledge of average, single-issue readership and of the number of different people who will see one or both of two different issues, it is possible to use these data to calibrate a suitable mathematical model which represents the build-up of audience across successive issues and thus to predict the numbers of people seeing two, three or any number of issues.

Looking directly at reading behaviour over several successive issues takes us into the area of continuous measurement amongst a constant panel of respondents, usually via a readership diary. Given that the diary record captures not only all the reading occasions for a particular newspaper or magazine but also which issue was seen on each occasion, then we may estimate reading frequency quite straightforwardly by comparing, over some period of time, the number of different issues looked at with the number actually published in that interval. We may, of course, have some reservations about the completeness and accuracy of the diary record; and we should also note that some considerable length of continuous measurement will be necessary: for example, given its frequency of publication, it may not be possible to draw any very firm conclusions about the frequency of readership of a monthly magazine in less than six months or a year. Further, people's reading does not have to keep exactly in step with the publication of successive issues and often does not do so; consequently, at the beginning of a readership diary record, we might think that the reading of some particular issue had not taken place, only to find it occurring later. These comments are intended merely to underline that, whilst a diary does, indeed, provide direct evidence of the frequency with which a title is read, that evidence needs to be interpreted with care.

By far the most common approach to reading frequency measurement, however, is to ask direct questions on the subject; but what questions? Should they relate to historical reading behaviour, in the recent past, or to what people 'usually' do? Should the alternative answers between which respondents must choose be couched in numbers, or in verbal terms, or in some mixture of the two? And how long a scale is best – how many different, possible answers should we offer?

A question phrased in terms of recent, actual behaviour might run, 'In the past month, how many different issues of *Elle* have you read or looked at?', with precoded answers comprising 'none', 'one', 'two', 'three' or 'four'. By contrast, a question relating to usual, habitual behaviour might be, 'In the average week, how many issues of the *Chicago Tribune* do you read these days?', with possible answers running from 'seven' down to 'one' and 'less than one' – this last category arising because, in talking about *habitual* behaviour, a reading frequency of less than once a week is logically possible.

In practice, the difference in the results obtained from these two approaches is not so great as might be imagined, principally because, however the question is worded, readers have a strong tendency to reply in terms of their perception of their *usual* behaviour, overlooking atypical events, even if they were quite recent. There is thus some merit in avoiding the somewhat spurious accuracy implied by asking, 'How many issues in the past week?' or 'month' or 'year' and, further, there is some advantage in offering low-frequency readers an opportunity to make a positive claim, if a small one, rather than forcing them into the choice between 'none' and 'one'.

Since reading frequency is (at first sight) a 'hard', quantitative measure, there has been considerable use of numerically phrased questions but, again, the accuracy thus conferred on the replies may be more apparent than real: to decide whether one's usual behaviour is nearer seeing three issues of a daily newspaper out of each four, or nearer four out of four is far from easy. In any case, as we shall see, numerical claims should not be taken at their face value.

Essentially, the objective of any well-formulated question on reading frequency should be seen as merely dividing readers into mutually exclusive groups, such that readers within any one group have reasonably similar probabilities of contact with the average issue, whilst the between-group averages differ clearly. In turn, this implies a question which allows readers easily and consistently to relate their own behaviour to one of the alternative answers offered them. A successful compromise is to phrase the question basically in verbal terms, but to offer numerical illustrations as anchor points. Thus we might ask, 'About how often do you see *Der Spiegel* these days – frequently (three or four issues out of every four), sometimes (one or two issues out of four) or only occasionally (less than one issue out of four)?'

On the question of how long a reading frequency scale it is best to use, a large volume of evidence (drawn from a far wider field of measurement theory than just readership research itself) supports the contention that modesty is the best policy. It might appear that the more numerous the different probabilities of contact with the average issue that may be allocated to any given reader, the more accurate must be the estimates of the net readership coverage of several issues or of the proportions of the population having the opportunity of contact with different numbers of ads. But such an assumption completely ignores any limitation on readers' ability consistently and accurately to relate their own behaviour to the possible answers. There are, unquestionably, twelve issues of a monthly magazine each year; but to offer a scale running from 'none out of twelve read in the past year' to 'twelve out of twelve' is grossly to overtax respondents' powers. Three-, four-and five-point scales well cover the range of practicable compromises between obtaining stable, reproducible data and mathematical precision in the application of the results.

So we may prefer a question on regularity of reading that relates to what people usually do, is couched in verbal/quantitative terms and proffers a limited range of possible replies. But can we take any numerical results that ensue at their face value? The answer is, categorically, 'no'; if we conduct methodological research to check the validity of the reading frequency claims we have obtained, we shall find that there is a tendency for regular readers to *over*-claim their frequency of contact with a newspaper or magazine (as I forgot the snowstorm which robbed me of *The Daily Telegram*), whilst low-frequency readers *under*-claim. The distortions may be considerable, but they will vary from survey to survey and from title to title; there is no simple, single straight-line relationship between 'real' frequency of reading and the claims that people make.

We are consequently forced back on using any reading frequency question in the mode just described – basically, to *categorise* readers, but no more – and appealing to other data to quantify the responses.

The most common route is to employ the average issue readership claims themselves. Consider a Recent-Reading-based survey, which included the three-point reading frequency scale illustrated earlier. Suppose that, of those respondents claiming to see *Newsweek* 'frequently', 78 per cent had read or looked at any issue in the past week, whilst the figures for those claiming to read 'sometimes' and 'only occasionally' were 53 per cent and 17 per cent, respectively. We should then argue that each person in the 'frequently' group had a probability of contact with the average issue of 0.78, and so on.

Whilst this line of calculation is widely employed, there are alternatives. In conjunction with the reading frequency claims themselves, other data from a survey may also be employed to segment respondents into groups to which different contact probabilities are attached. Alternatively, we might calibrate reading frequency claims by recourse to research entirely separate from the main readership survey; for example, we might (purely for this purpose) run a readership diary panel for a period and, when signing-up people to this panel, put to them the frequency questions we intended later to use in our main research. The diary data could then be employed to calibrate the claims made at the initial, sign-up interview.

Finally in this section, it is necessary to make some comment about the potential use of frequency of reading results as a basis for estimating average issue readership itself. The method may be self-evident and is very simple: if we asked, 'Out of each six issues of *The Sowetan* that are published in a week, how many do you usually read?', then we can go on to argue that, of those claiming 'one', one-sixth will see the average issue, together with a third of those saying 'two', and so on. Adding these products together thus yields an AIR estimate. However, whilst this approach has been employed and whilst its logic is impeccable, the very severe qualifications that must be placed on numerical, face-value frequency claims cripple its potential accuracy. But if one chose first to calibrate the claims by some separate, robust technique, that would be a different matter.

THE EUROPEAN SCENE

Despite the impact of television on print media advertising revenue, readership research in Europe is alive and extremely well. Erhard Meier's *Summary of Current Readership Research*, as updated for the fifth world-wide symposium in Hong Kong in February 1991, listed no fewer than 24 continuous or regular surveys, across 16 countries. (We are here extending the definition of 'Europe' slightly so as to include both Turkey to the East and the Republic of Ireland to the West.) Together, these surveys account for well over half a million interviews annually.

Two main features characterise this European scene, one organisational and one methodological.

There are three basic ways in which national readership surveys may be organised and administered. In the first mode, an 'industry body' is set up (often, but not necessarily, on a non-profit basis), ideally representing the interests of all three sides of the industry: publishers, advertisers and their agencies. This body controls the specification and financing of the survey, directly commissioning the research from one or more suppliers, often via a tendering process. The industry body involves itself, to a greater or lesser degree, in all aspects of methodology, research production and data dissemination.

In the second mode, the research is sponsored jointly by a number of individual companies, who may be publishers, advertisers or agencies. Whilst they come together out of common interests, they cannot be said necessarily to be representative of the industry sector or sectors from which they are drawn; in this mode, there is far less *independent* control of the design, execution and reporting of the research.

The third alternative is for a market research company entrepreneurially to propose a readership survey, to be solely responsible for its design and execution and either to solicit sponsorship *a priori* on a 'multi-client' basis or to sell the data to whom it may, once the research is completed. There is here no 'industry' control at all, apart from regulation via any professional code of conduct for market research that may exist in the country concerned.

Historically, the first of these organisational modes has held considerable sway, with a number of the bodies concerned now well over 25 years old. Currently, there are industry contracts for readership research in Belgium, Germany, Great Britain, the Irish Republic, the Netherlands and Switzerland.

The second clearly pronounced feature of the European readership research scene is an adherence to the Recent Reading approach for estimating average issue readership which originated in Britain, as has been noted, prior to the Second World War: it applies for 13 out of the 24 surveys mentioned earlier.

Care should be taken in interpreting the departures from this pattern; where 'frequency' is listed in the table, it certainly does not imply that, in those surveys, people's numerical claims as to their regularity of reading are taken at face value. Rather, in most of these cases, a reading frequency scale (together, sometimes, with extensive, other data, as in Germany) will be used as a basis for segmenting readers into a number of cohesive groups such that, between groups, there is a difference in the ratio of the number of people reading a publication within the publication interval to the number claiming 'ever' to read that title. A specific 'reading probability', varying between the groups, is then applied to all members of a given group, title by title. Thus, whilst the reading frequency claims are, indeed, used, their calibration and the consequent production of an 'average issue readership' estimate depends on other data.

Where there has been a clear-cut departure from the basic Recent Reading approach, however, is in those countries who employed it earlier but who have jettisoned it in favour of First Reading Yesterday: the Netherlands, initially, then followed by Denmark and, latterly, Norway. Note, though, that the questioning in these surveys (as we explained in the earlier section on basic methods) is still in terms of '*any* issue'; there is not a single European country that relies, or has relied, on specific-issue-recognition, Through-the-Book methods.

READERSHIP MEASUREMENT IN BRITAIN

Readership measurement in Britain now has a history of over 60 years. However, a number of the very early surveys of newspapers and magazines were, in fact, devoted to circulation rather than readership as here understood and took as their unit of analysis the household rather than the individual. Examples are provided by *Press Circulations Analysed* from the London Research Bureau (LRB) in 1928; circulation-related surveys by the LRB for the Institute of Incorporated Practitioners in Advertising (IIPA) in 1930, 1931 and 1932; *Investigating Press Circulations* from Repfords, also in 1932; and (despite its misleading title) *The Readership of Newspapers and Periodicals* from the Incorporated Society of British Advertisers in 1936.

It seems probable that the earliest British, formal research into individuals' readership was carried out by Gallup for J. Walter Thompson (JWT) in 1932, followed by research from the London Press Exchange – a leading advertising agency – in 1934 and another JWT survey in 1938. Without question, however, readership research methods and principles that would be readily recognised today were exemplified in the IIPA's *Survey of Press Readership*, undertaken in 1939.

During the Second World War, newspaper reading was of equal interest to sociologists and to the coalition government of the day. That period saw the publication of *Newspaper Reading in the Third Year of the War* by Allen & Unwin; *Newspapers and the Public*, from the Central Office of Information in 1943; and surveys by Mass-Observation in 1941, 1942 and 1944 and by the British Institute of Public Opinion (Gallup Poll Ltd), also in 1944.

The year 1947 saw the publication of research from Attwood Statistics, of another *Survey of Press Readership* by the IIPA and of the first of the *Hulton Readership Surveys* from the Hulton Press, home of what was probably Britain's most famous illustrated weekly, *Picture Post*.

The Hulton series was to continue until 1954, when the IIPA took over responsibility for the design, commissioning and publication of regular surveys – although their financing, then as now, was largely in the hands of the press; the meetings held annually for the purposes of negotiating the funding could be stormy – and often were.

From this research initiated by the IIPA just before the Second World War grew the present-day series of National Readership Surveys. Within this chapter, it would be quite impracticable even to sketch the total history of the National Readership Survey (NRS) over that period, particularly as regards the very large volume of experimental and methodological work that has been carried out to guide the NRS's growth and development; but the proceedings of the first International Symposium provide a reasonably full account of this British history, as well as descriptions of readership research development in other countries. Here, we can only signpost the major changes the NRS has undergone, before describing its present format.

From the outset, the NRS has employed the Recent Reading technique, as did the preceding Hulton research. In the early 1960s, alternative techniques were, for a time, under consideration: a modification of Recent Reading, using recall periods no longer than a week; Through-the-Book; and the estimation of average issue readership on the basis of reading frequency claims. Two events prompted this reconsideration: a landmark study by Dr William Belson, published as *Studies in Readership*, which demonstrated considerable limitations on people's ability accurately to report when they had last read a publication; and work on the extent of 'model bias'. However, no basic change was adopted and all further British efforts have concentrated on improving the accuracy of Recent-Reading-based estimates.

At the inception of the NRS, its sole objective was to estimate average issue readership and, consequently, the only critical questions in the interview were those to establish when an issue of a publication had most recently been seen. However, experimental measurement of regularity of readership commenced in 1962 and, by May 1965, a 'reading frequency' question had become a constant feature of the Survey, although it was applied only to the major titles in the NRS's media list, not to all of them.

In the latter half of the 1960s, attention turned to refinement of the concept of average *issue* readership and to the possibility of providing NRS users with information on 'intensity' of readership. An extensive research programme led to the development and testing of the so-called 'Picture Scale', comprising illustrations of issues of an imaginary publication with different proportions of their pages coloured red; in respect of each publication seen, each respondent had to say which picture best represented their usual within-the-issue reading behaviour.

A year of major change for the NRS was 1968, both technically and administratively. The readership section of the interview was already lengthy, involving a preliminary 'read in the last three months' question for 83 titles, which served solely as a filter; measurement of 'when last read' for, on average, the 20 publications that passed the filter; and collection of reading frequency data for 38 titles. With the desire to capture yet more data but with the possibility of interview overload also in mind, a new format was successfully tested and introduced from the beginning of 1968. The reading frequency question, now asked for all titles, was moved to the head of the interview, serving both to provide data in its own right and to act as a filter – a person claiming zero reading frequency for a given newspaper or magazine was not questioned further on that title; the 'when last read' section followed; and the Picture Scale came last in the readership portion of the total questionnaire. At the same time, the NRS sample was increased from approximately 16,000 per annum to 30,000, both to allow analysis in terms of smaller subgroups of the population and to permit more frequent data publication.

Administratively, 1968 saw the switch of responsibility for the NRS Survey from the IPA – which had by then carried out sterling work over more than 30 years – to the newly formed Joint Industry Committee for National Readership Surveys, representing the publishers (through the Newspaper Publishers Association and the Periodical Publishers Association), the agencies (through the IPA) and the advertisers (through the Incorporated Society of British Advertisers). Early features of JICNARS were an independent chairman, a permanent secretariat, standing technical and finance sub-committees and a technical director.

Between 1968 and 1984, a great deal of further experimental work was conducted; the Picture Scale was dropped in 1972, mainly on the grounds of new evidence of the limited ability of its scores to predict the actual extent of within-the-issue reading and of the modest differences between the data for one publication and another, but otherwise, no major changes occurred. However, throughout the latter part of this period, pressures increased to widen the NRS's coverage, particularly as regards smaller and more specialised magazines. But given interview length as it then stood, it was clear that no such extension could be accommodated without another basic change to the NRS interview's structure. Consequently, the latest version – the Extended Media List (EML) questionnaire was devised, tested and introduced from 1985.

The principal feature that distinguished the EML version of the NRS questionnaire from its predecessors was that respondents were first shown the titles of *groups* of publications and asked whether, in the past year, they had read any of the newspapers or magazines in a particular group; only if a person replied 'yes' were they then questioned, in detail, about their recent reading – and frequency of reading – of each separate publication in that group. Self-evidently, this approach allowed the presentation of a far longer media list, and the quicker filtering-out of irrelevant titles than had been the case when they were presented singly, as in all previous versions of the NRS.

It is necessary to note but two more changes to the NRS – one organisational and one technical, but both of considerable importance – before turning to the details of the Survey as it now stands.

The pattern of 'industry' readership research, as enshrined in the formation and structure of JICNARS, had not only served the British market well for nearly 25 years but, as we have seen, had provided a model for numerous other countries' surveys. However, it came to be felt by some that perhaps JICNARS had outlived its usefulness; that its structures and particularly the considerable role of its technical sub-committee no longer best served the clear-cut communication of the needs of NRS data users (and particularly publishers); and that the existence of JICNARS did not make for the speediest adaptation of the Survey to changes in market-place needs. Consequently, during 1991, the technical sub-committee was abolished, virtually overnight and with it went the various working parties and study groups that had been a feature of the JICNARS scene for so long. Then, from the beginning of 1992, National Readership Surveys Ltd replaced JICNARS, with a board purposefully smaller in size than had been the Committee.

In parallel with the planning and implementation of these organisational changes, 1991 had seen considerable experimentation with Computer Assisted Personal Interviewing (CAPI) as a means of readership data capture, an alternative to the pencil-and-paper questionnaire which had been in use since the start of the NRS. The tenders invited for a new NRS contract, to run from 1992, covered the possibility of a change to this methodology; a successful test was completed in late 1991 and the Survey 'went CAPI' from 1 July 1992. In the detailed description of the NRS that follows, therefore, the pencil-and-paper EML questionnaire is first described, before the changes that CAPI occasioned are noted.

Sampling

The universe that the NRS sample represents comprises adults of age 15 years and older resident in private households and at some (but not all) types of institutional address, throughout Great Britain. Two major changes to the method of sampling this universe were introduced from 1992: as a sampling frame, the Postcode Address File (PAF) replaced the Electoral Register; and disproportional sampling was introduced. The first of these changes resulted from the deteriorating coverage of the universe by the Electoral Register, in part attributable to the introduction of the Community Charge and the purposeful failure to register by a sizeable proportion of adults, particularly in Scotland. Disproportional sampling

aimed to over-represent certain population subgroups that were of above-average importance as advertising targets.
The NRS employs a stratified, multistage probability sampling design. The current, 1993 sample size is 37,500.

The interview

From 1984 until the introduction of Computer Assisted Personal Interviewing in July 1992, the NRS used the pencil-and-paper EML questionnaire.
Critical to its measurement of readership are the aids used to prompt respondents. These comprise cards showing, on their fronts, a listing of up to seven newspaper or magazine titles, in uniform typography and, on the reverse of the cards, the same publications, but now as 'mastheads' or logos, together with the relevant frequency of publication. At the foot of this reverse side of each card is a scale of reading frequency, running from 'ALMOST ALWAYS At least 2 issues out of 4' to 'NOT IN THE PAST YEAR'. There are somewhat under 50 different cards in current use; each is printed in two versions, between which the positioning of the titles on the card varies. The rotation plan depends on the number of titles a card shows.
Sorting the cards into numerical order, the interviewer says:

We want to find out about the newspapers and magazines you have read at all in the past year. I should like you to look through each of these cards in turn. As soon as you see any publication on a card that you remember reading *at any time* in the past year, please put the card on this pile. If you are sure you have not read any of the publications on a card in the past year, please put that card here. If you're not sure about a card, put it aside and we shall come back to it later.

The interviewer explains that it does not matter who bought the copy that was read, where it was seen or how old it was. 'Just as long as you can remember spending a couple of minutes reading or looking at *any* of the publications on a card in the past year it goes on this pile.'
The cards are presented in one of two orders: daily newspapers are taken first and Sundays last, or *vice versa*, the magazines coming between these groups in 'forward' or 'reverse' sequence. When they have all been sorted, the 'not sure' ones are rechecked and the respondent is then given a final chance to go through the cards put on the 'no' pile, to make sure they contain no titles that *have* been seen in the past year.
The 'yes' cards are then sorted back into numerical order and the

interviewer asks, taking each such card in turn and showing its reverse side: 'Which of these newspapers [or magazines] do you read or look at almost always? ... Which do you read or look at quite often? ... And which have you read or looked at only occasionally in the past year?' For each title not yet mentioned, the respondent is then asked, 'Have you read or looked at any issue of ... in the past year?' and, if the answer is 'yes', 'Would that be almost always ... quite often ... only occasionally?'

Finally in the main readership section of the questionnaire, the all-important timing of the most recent reading event is established. With the respondent still looking at the same card, the interviewer asks, 'Which, if any, of these newspapers [or magazines] did you read or look at yesterday?', substituting 'Saturday' for 'yesterday' in the case of interviews taking place on a Monday; 'Which others have you read or looked at on or since ...day?', naming the day a week ago; and, for each title not yet mentioned 'When did you last read or look at any copy of ... [apart from today]?'

The EML version of the NRS questionnaire then goes on to cover a number of other topics: readership of newly launched titles, measured more simply; readership of local weekly newspapers, measured generically, rather than title-by-title; use of local directories; cinema-going; radio listening and TV viewing; responsibility for food and grocery shopping; shopping expenditure; and the demographic classification of the individual and of their household, in very considerable detail.

In addition to this main questionnaire, there was also (prior to the change to CAPI) a supplementary section, completed by the respondent but under the interviewer's supervision, which had the advantages of extending the data collected without perceptibly lengthening the interview, and of fitting into time in which the interviewer could also use to complete other, administrative tasks. It, too, covered a variety of areas: the frequency of readership of different topics featured in newspapers; consumption of alcoholic drinks; leisure activities; motoring; holidays; business air travel; telephone possession; consumer durables; personal and household plans; education; qualifications; and financial services and arrangements.

The introduction of Computer Assisted Personal Interviewing has brought some small changes to the readership section of the questionnaire. The prompt cards having been initially sorted by the respondent and the 'no' cards rechecked, readership in the past year is next measured for *each* title on any card screened-in as containing one or more publications read in that period. For each newspaper or magazine claimed as having been seen in the past year, questioning on when reading most recently took place now precedes the question on frequency of reading, rather than following it, as was the case in the pencil-and-paper questionnaire. Further, separate identification of 'yesterday' reading now applies only to daily newspapers. For these titles, the CAPI questionnaire goes on to establish when last any Saturday edition was seen and how frequently such editions are read.

The change to computer-assisted interviewing has also led to the abolition of the separate, self-completed questionnaire. Its topics are still covered, but the respondent is provided with a prompt showing merely the questions and the codes for different, possible answers. These codes he or she calls out, the data being entered directly on the keyboard by the interviewer.

Data analysis

Following fieldwork, National Readership Survey results are subject to extensive reweighting and, in the event of abnormal newspaper or magazine publishing circumstances, adjustment. Weighting *per se* may be seen as proceeding in two stages.

First applied is a set of 'pre-weights', necessary to compensate for purposeful departures from allocating an equal probability of selection to each and every informant. These weights cover unequal sampling fractions for respondents within households; the constraint of the number of sampling points per sub-area to be a multiple of 12; and some over-sampling in Scotland and in parts of England and Wales, such as to provide adequate sub-samples in the circulation areas of certain regional newspapers.

The second stage of weighting corrects for discrepancies between the demographic profile of the achieved sample and that of the population and is carried out monthly. First, 84 cells are defined in terms of sex, six age groups and seven survey regions; the weight applied to the informants in any one cell depends on the profiles of both the current month's and of the previous year's samples. The resultant data are then rim-weighted by sex within age and sex within groupings of areas; at this stage, the 15–24 age group is split into 15–17 and 18–24 subgroups. These procedures produce an initial estimate of the distribution of social grade within sex. This estimate is combined with that from the previous month to produce new, exponentially smoothed estimates of target proportions of grade within sex. Finally, the data are rim-weighted again by sex within age group, sex within area grouping and sex within social grade.

Quite apart from being reweighted as just described, NRS data are also adjusted to compensate for any material loss of circulation by a newspaper or magazine during the survey period as a result, for example, of industrial action. In detail, the adjustment procedures are quite complex, but their basis is to accept as valid the reading *frequency* claims made during some affected period and then to derive, on the basis of a prior, 'normal' timespan, the ratio of the numbers of informants reading the title in question during the issue period (e.g. the seven days preceding the interview for a weekly magazine) to the numbers claiming each possible frequency of reading that title.

CATEGORISING READERS AND READING EVENTS

This chapter has, so far, been very largely concerned with the basic problems of measuring average issue readership and reading frequency; but the typical survey will contain much, much more besides and to these other measures we now briefly turn. They fall into two main groups: measures aiming to qualify the *individual*, the reader; and measures aiming to add information on the *reading event* or on the interrelationship between reader and publication.

The reader

Since the main application of readership survey results will be in the selection of newspapers and magazines as advertising vehicles, the detailed categorisation of readers will, obviously, be of considerable importance, since different sorts of people may vary widely in their value as prospective customers for a given product or service. The most traditional and longest-serving categorisations are the demographic ones, so that readers (like so many of us) will not only be 'broken down by sex and age', but also by many other trusty classifiers, such as social class, occupation, income, educational level, household composition and tenure.

Today, however, in readership research as elsewhere, demographics may well not be seen as sufficient; there may be a call additionally to classify readers geodemographically or pyschographically or in terms of their purchasing behaviour. Any detailed discussion of the merits and demerits of alternative schema of consumer classification or of target-group definition would be out of place here, since these questions have no direct or unique relationship to the problems of measuring readership; but there is one general problem whenever the call is materially to widen the coverage of a readership survey and to add considerably to the data collected.

As mentioned above, the sheer weight of the number of publications to be covered in a single survey will often be onerous, and very detailed and careful questioning on readership itself is called for, which will be unavoidably repetitious, to some degree at least. Any survey must, furthermore, contain a raft of basic, demographic, classification questions; and many questionnaires will make at least a nod towards other topics, such as the possession of a range of durable goods or contact with media other than newspapers and magazines. Consequently, a lengthy and demanding interview is almost guaranteed, even before detailed survey planning starts.

Such circumstances just do not permit the further addition, within the readership survey interview of, say, the battery of scales necessary for a thorough and satisfactory psychographic segmentation of the sample or the volume of questioning necessary to establish purchasing behaviour, at the brand level, over a wide range of product fields. (It is to be borne in mind that few if any readership surveys are conducted for a single client or in the context of media choice decision-taking just in one area; their results are expected to be of applicability across a wide range of circumstances.)

There are two solutions to this data overload enigma. On the one hand, the problem may be stood on its head: instead of trying to expand a *readership* survey satisfactorily to cover, say, the purchasing of packaged goods, basic questions on newspapers and magazines may be added to research that was tailor-made to measure what people buy. Such a solution can be moderately successful; but it is unlikely that any simplified, abbreviated set of questions will go far towards providing unbiased, precise estimates of average issue readership (and particularly so if the other research vehicle involves a self-completion questionnaire).

Alternatively, we may try to obtain the best of both worlds, retaining two quite separate surveys optimally designed for different purposes – one to estimate readership, the other to capture quite different data – and then invoke data fusion. This is a statistical technique applied to two quite separate databases, often comprising the results from independent research on separate samples, so conducted that the two questionnaires partly overlap. Its objective is to 'donate' information resident only in one survey to the respondents of the other, using characteristics measured in both samples as a link, such that the end result is as if *all* the questions had been asked of *all* the people. To an extent, the legitimacy and limitations of data fusion remain a matter of theoretical debate, but in practice the procedures may be shown to produce eminently usable and useful results. So, for example, in the present context, a readership survey might be carried out and, quite separately, another sample might be categorised in terms of their values and lifestyles. Data fusion could then produce a third, simulated 'sample', fully open to further analysis, as if the readership survey respondents had themselves been subjected to the values-and-lifestyles questions' battery.

The reading event

The reasons for which such information is seen as being of value are twofold. Given that 'all average issue readers are equal, but some are more equal than others', they may differ between themselves in two distinct ways: in their thoroughness of within-the-issue readership, and thus on their likelihood of contact with an ad the issue contains, conditional on seeing the issue at all in the first place; or they may differ in the 'closeness' of their relationship with the newspaper or magazine concerned and thus (possibly) in the effect its contents (including advertisements) may have on them.

It is unquestionably true that, within any group of people that a survey uniformly classifies as 'average issue readers' (or as having an equal probability of contact with the average issue), there will be person-to-person variations in what is commonly referred to as 'thoroughness' or 'intensity' of readership; and it is equally true that there are a whole host of measurable characteristics of readers which are predictive (to a greater or lesser extent) of such variations in reading intensity. The data which are most commonly collected under this heading include the source of the copy a reader sees (bought copies may be consumed more thoroughly than passed-on or casually encountered ones); where reading takes place (in-home reading may be more intense than that which accompanies commuting); the timing and circumstances of reading (a magazine filling an office lunch-hour may be approached differently from one taken to bed, last thing at night); the total time spent with an issue, from when it is first read to its final discarding; the number of separate occasions on which an issue is picked up (or the number of different days on which it is read); and the proportion of the issue which is read or looked at (with the question worded, for example, in terms of the percentage of total pages that are looked at).

In all of these cases, it is possible to phrase questions to measure one or another characteristic of the reading event, and the answers obtained not only have face validity but may actually be demonstrated to be relevant. Such validation is often approached by taking people through an issue they claim to have seen before and asking, page by page, which items they read or looked at. Whilst such 'page traffic' measurement will never be perfect – given the vagaries of memories and other biasing factors – it will be found, for example, that in-home readers, or those who say they personally purchased the copy they read, will report an above-average proportion of pages as containing something they have seen. There are, however, three qualifications we should note on the usefulness of these sorts of measures.

First, there is a great deal of correlation between these features, and therefore redundancy of information, if two or more of these questions are asked. Indeed, there is probably only one underlying dimension, which we might label 'affinity': the 'closer' a reader is to a publication, the more likely are they to obtain their own copies, to read them over an extended period, to pick them up several times, to open every page, and so on.

Second, frequency of readership (which will almost certainly be measured, for different purposes) is itself a strong correlate of 'affinity': regular, frequent readers value the newspaper or magazine concerned and read it thoroughly. Thus it may be questioned how much *more* information is gained from first estimating regularity of reading and then measuring additionally, say, source of copy.

Third, to include any such questions as these is of little practical value unless their results are very fully integrated with a readership survey's other, basic findings. Looking ahead a little to the application of readership findings, we could imagine a user faced with this problem: 'Per advertising pound, this magazine yields me 1,250 relevant readers and that one 1,500; but in the former audience, 40 per cent are in-home readers, whilst the figure is only 30 per cent for the latter publication. Which should I choose?' Faced with such an unresolved trade-off, the outcome may all too easily be for the survey user to throw away the expensively collected, subsidiary data on place of reading.

The measures discussed so far in this section may be thought of, collectively, as *indirect* predictors of intensity of readership or of within-the-issue reading behaviour. Such intensity has two essential dimensions: the number of times an issue is picked up, and the proportion of the issue which is looked at on each such reading occasion. Within a readership survey interview – or separately – we may also attempt to measure these dimensions directly. A typical sequence of questioning would establish how many different issues of a publication were looked at 'yesterday' (the day preceding the interview); for each reading event, whether that issue had been seen *before* 'yesterday'; and what proportion of pages was looked at, on average, per reading event. Reading-days-per-person-per-issue may then be estimated from the ratio of 'total reading events yesterday' to '*first* readings yesterday'; and this figure, multiplied by the fraction of the issue seen per reading occasion yields an estimate of the average number of exposures per page per reader, usually known as a Magazine Page Exposure (MPX) score. (The technique is, in principle, equally applicable to newspapers but numbers of reading days are then far less relevant). Whilst collection of MPX data is an ongoing feature of the two main American surveys of magazine readership and has been undertaken *ad hoc* in a number of European countries, the numbers of page exposures have not, so far, tended to supplant average issue readership as the main unit of comparative measurement.

Turning now to measurements which bear not so much on the character of the reading event but more on the relationship between reader and publication, the philosophy behind the research is entirely different (although not always clear-headedly seen as such). Two new, implicit assumptions are now being made: that 'affinity' has implications not only for the quantitative *probability* of contact between reader and ad, conditional on issue readership, but also for the ad's effect and effectiveness; and that there will be differences between readers and between publications.

Approaches to measuring the 'closeness' of the reader–publication relationship can vary from the use of a single, simple question such as, 'How concerned would you be if this magazine ceased publication?' to employing extremely lengthy question batteries, covering both reading behaviour and attitudes towards publications, with subsequent, sophisticated mathematical analysis in pursuit of one or more underlying dimensions. However, the interpretation of the evidence that has been offered in support of the *relevance* of such measures is much more disputatious; there is by no means general agreement that 'affinity', as here defined, correlates with the communication effect an ad achieves (all else held constant) or with the results of such communication on the readers' attitudes and behaviour towards the advertised brand or product.

DATA DISSEMINATION AND DATA USE

Many users of readership survey findings still rely solely on conventional, hard-copy reports so that, in this area of research, printed tables have by no means been driven out by electronic publication. But, in any country, the existence of a sizeable, regular, generally accepted survey will almost certainly mean that one or more computer bureaux find it commercially worthwhile to offer an on-line analysis service; batch processing still exists but is of decreasing importance. Major publishers may choose to offer their own analysis service, on- or off-line, or to subsidise the cost of bureau runs, partly or wholly, when analyses are commissioned by potential advertisers or their agencies. Finally here, the dissemination of readership survey data on diskette is growing, with the data then handled, on users' own disks, using either multipurpose cross-tabulation programs or software specially created with the commoner forms of analysis of readership results in mind.

The frequency of readership data release – whether in hard-copy format or otherwise – may sometimes represent a not altogether happy compromise. When the media marketplace is active – at times of the launch of new titles, for example, the demise of others or of relatively steep trends in circulation – publishers, in particular, will seek frequent access to up-to-date readership estimates for the purposes of competitive marketing of their titles; but such demands are not always well-met by available sample sizes. A decade ago in Britain, annual or six-monthly reports would have been seen as fully adequate; today (with an annual sample of 37,500), there is a strong demand for quarterly or monthly data. Statistical smoothing techniques may be specially employed to remove the worst of spurious, short-term variations in estimated readership levels, but may not provide a complete answer to the problem.

In printed reports, there are a limited number of types of basic readership data tables which constantly recur.

First and most important are tabulations of *readership penetration* – that is to say average issue readership, title by title, shown in absolute terms and as a percentage of the population.

Penetration figures will be reported for the total population and for a whole range of subgroups, defined both demographically (by age, by social class or income and by geographical area, for example) and in terms of other data collected on the survey which identify commonly employed target groups – 'mothers with children under 5', say, or 'freezer owners'. Often, the fineness of the breakdowns will be further enhanced by including separate sets of tables for each of the main population subgroups – for example, 'men', 'women', 'housewives' and 'heads-of-household'.

The second main category comprises *readership profile* tables. Here, the data are rearranged such that the total average issue readership of each title becomes the base, whilst the body of the table shows the breakdown or 'profile' of this total audience across subgroups of interest. Note that, in profile tables, since the base for each publication's breakdown is the (unweighted) number of readers rather than the survey's total sample or some constant sub-sample, confidence limits of similarly sized percentages may vary quite considerably, when they occur in different lines.

Next, most survey reports will contain tabular data on *reading frequency* and/or *cumulative readership*. For Recent-Reading-based surveys employing a separate reading frequency question, two formats are common: to tabulate, title by title, the probabilities of contact with the average issue that correspond to each separate point on the particular reading frequency scale used; and to show the cumulative coverage for each number of issues between two and, say, ten or twelve – the estimated number of different people, that is, who will read at least one issue amongst the stated number. These latter, cumulative coverage data, of course, need to be modelled; they cannot be obtained directly from the survey's findings, just by tabulation. Commonly, a binomial expansion will be used, in conjunction with the probabilities of contact with the average issue. If this is the case, note that an implicit assumption has been made that the probabilities of the same person reading two different issues of the same newspaper or magazine are independent.

Printed reports will often be completed by a set of *readership duplication* tables, showing what proportion of the average issue readership of publication A are also in the audience of publication B, for all possible pairs of the total number of newspapers and magazines the survey covers. Clearly, overlap between audiences is not just confined to pairs of publications and it may be of considerable interest to a user of the data to know how net coverage increases when a third, fourth or fifth title is added. To show results for all possible combinations of titles would be quite impossible, given the survey has a media list of any length. Earlier in readership research history, it was quite common to tabulate audience data for a limited number of 'typical' combinations of different titles, but easy access to cheap computing has largely obviated the need for such tables.

How are readership data actually used, whether working from the page of a printed report or from a computer's disk? In answering this question, we shall ignore the somewhat secondary, editorial application of the results (for the purposes of monitoring and developing a newspaper or magazine as a product) and concentrate on the advertising area; but here, a difference in viewpoint must be recognised as between publishers (often a survey's main paymasters) on the one hand and, on the other, advertisers and their agencies. The publisher's concern is how his particular publication is positioned, according to its readership results, in the market for advertising space sales. The advertiser or agency, by contrast, is seeking the most cost-effective route to a particular advertising goal; the choice of individual publications is but a means to an end and it is their combined effectiveness, in a schedule, which is of most importance.

To arrive, finally, at an advertising schedule comprising varying numbers of ads in several publications, the task of the advertiser or agency will comprise several successive stages: deciding whether print media should be used at all; if so, selecting a list of 'candidate' publications; from this, constructing a schedule; and checking the forecast performance of that schedule. Whilst we cannot, here, hope to develop at all fully the media planning process and the considerations that will be involved, it should be borne in mind that the decisions just listed are to be taken in the context of defined marketing and advertising goals, of a stated target group (or of different importance-as-customers weights across different parts of the population) and of the development of the creative content of the advertising, from which media choice cannot and certainly should not be divorced.

Except in some extreme and exceptional cases, readership research results are of little relevance to the *inter*-media decision – the choice, that is, of what proportion of the advertising budget should be devoted to newspapers or magazines, as contrasted with television, coupons, radio, competitions, posters, on-pack offers, the cinema, sky-writing or any other medium. The main reason is that, whilst audience numbers provide an effective trading currency within each medium, the exchange rate *between* the currencies is ill-defined: what are the relative values of having a specific prospective customer in front of a 30-second commercial and in front of a full-colour, full-page magazine ad?

The decision having been taken to use print media (mainly on grounds, most probably, other than the evidence of the audience data), a first list of possible publications may be drawn up, having regard to their coverage of the relevant target group, the concentration of their readership within that group (as seen in the profile tables) and their rates; quite probably, the computer will be asked to 'cost-rank' these candidate vehicles, dividing the insertion cost for each by the relevant audience and listing the publications in the ascending order of the ratio. Note that the information on advertising rates is external to the readership research, of course; its use is not absolutely straightforward, due to the dependence of costs on ad size and the need to decide what sizes are 'equivalent': if, for example, full-page ads are to be taken in a tabloid newspaper, is the comparable cost for a broadsheet paper also the rate for the (larger) full page, or for some fraction of it?

The readership results can give some guidance on how many candidate publications it is necessary to consider, by showing whether just one or two titles reach virtually all the people in the target group and, if not, by reference to duplication data, which other publications will best increase the coverage. However, a whole host of other considerations will also enter into this decision; for example, it may be seen as desirable to use several different publications simply because their varying editorial contents best match different ads within the total campaign.

At this early stage of selecting a set of candidate publications, and later in the media selection process, the impression should not be conveyed that the decisions taken rest *solely* on readership research data, together with advertising rates. Other factors, often of an innately qualitative nature, will often be taken into account – and one of the most difficult facets of the profitable application of a survey's results is the logic of combining them with these other factors. For example, in drawing up a candidate list of magazines to carry a campaign for a range of instant meals, with the foodstuffs illustrated in full colour, most media planners would agree that relevant considerations would include the qualities of the paper on which a magazine was printed and of its colour reproduction; but even if the titles can, judgementally, be ranked on these criterion, what then is the trade-off, say, between a magazine being ranked second but displaying a 10 per cent advantage in terms of cost-per-thousand-relevant-readers?

A list of candidate publications agreed, a schedule is then to be constructed – that is to say, the number of ads to be placed in each publication is to be decided, subject to the available budget as a constraint. Today, this stage will most often be undertaken manually; probably several different schedules will be drawn up, all affordable but differing between themselves, to a greater or lesser degree, in the allocation of ads to publications, and the computer will then be employed to show the performance of each alternative schedule. Comparison of these outputs will lead to a final choice, perhaps with a little further fine tuning. However, there do exist programs which effect schedule construction and, with some qualifications, 'optimise' the choice of titles and of the numbers of ads to be placed in each. Such programs had a considerable vogue in the 1960s and 1970s, but are in much less frequent demand today.

An optimisation program requires as its input readership survey results; a list of newspapers and magazines, covered by the survey, amongst which a choice is to be made; the budget; the cost of advertising in each candidate vehicle; optionally, sets of 'market weights' and 'media weights'; and a 'response function'.

Market weights are ones attached to survey respondents to reflect their varying values as advertising prospects, on the basis of empirical data (such as their rates of purchasing the advertised product) or of judgement. Definition of what sorts of people comprise a 'target group' is equivalent to allocating a weight of one to those within this group and of zero to all others. *Media weights* are varied between the newspapers and magazines on the candidate list and aim to reflect their varying values (for the advertising campaign under consideration) on criteria other than audience size, audience composition and cost. When considering optimisation, it is of some importance to know how the program uses these weights: their effect may be to alter the probability of a particular person seeing the average issue of a given title; or they may actually 'weigh up' the impacts delivered by one publication, relative to another.

The response function presents the largest problems: it aims to represent the relative value of successive impacts on the same person. If no function is specified, many optimisation programs will assume that, for some particular reader, the first exposure to an ad in the campaign, the tenth and the hundredth all have equal value; but many planners would challenge such an assumption. However, empirical evidence on what 'shape' of response should be correctly assumed is sketchy and not always consistent; almost certainly, the function will vary from case to case, depending on aspects of the product field and brand, of purchasing patterns, of advertising content and of competitive campaigns. The lack of any very defensible solution to the response function problem has been amongst the reasons for declining faith in the utility of optimisation programs.

Subject to the above qualifications, an optimisation program then sets out to maximise the number of market-, media- and response-function-weighted impacts (contacts, that is, between a reader and a publication). By contrast, a schedule assessment program takes a 'ready-made' schedule and calculates the pattern of impacts it will deliver, showing, in particular, their distribution across the target group – the number of people having one opportunity to see an ad, two opportunities, three and so on. Such programs are in extensive use for the application of readership survey data; many will allow market and media weights to be used and will quickly answer 'what if?' questions, such as, 'What would happen to the pattern of impacts if we took two ads out of this magazine and put them into that one?'

PROMISES AND PITFALLS

Whatever approach is finally selected, there are certain features of readership survey design that are of paramount importance.

Usually, the list of publications to be measured will be a relatively long one and there will be a strong temptation to insert a preliminary, filter question, such that people are only subsequently questioned in relation to titles of which they have some knowledge or with which they have more than minimal contact. If possible, it is unquestionably preferable *not* to employ such a question. Unavoidably, some genuine readers – even if only a small proportion – will be erroneously 'filtered-out' and thus have no chance, later in the interview, correctly to contribute to the average issue readership estimate. (On the other side of this coin, the only argument sometimes advanced in favour of a filter question is that, if there is any danger of some respondents erroneously claiming readership of a publication because so doing accords them better status in the interviewer's eyes, then it is better that such inflated claims should occur at a relatively early and harmless stage of the interview.)

If a filter question is used, it must not relatively favour one publication, or one group of titles, over another. For example, a typical procedure might be to filter out those newspapers and magazines which a person claims not to have read or looked at 'In the past year'. However, a relatively infrequent reader of a weekly magazine would then have a considerably greater chance of being 'filtered-in' (or 'screened-in', in American terminology) than if the publication concerned were a monthly, simply because of the relative number of copies appearing in the filter period of a year.

Titles can be confused – sometimes very easily (remember our dear lady with *Woman* and *Woman's Own*?); to minimise such confusion is vital. The form of memory aid that is used is probably not of such vital importance as is sometimes alleged; using coloured illustrations of publications' logos, rather than black-and-white ones, or showing them in their correct relative sizes may make a difference, but not always and not equally for all titles. What is essential, however, is that the pace of the interview is carefully controlled, so that a respondent gives adequate and equal consideration to each prompt that is shown, before coming to a 'read' or 'not read' decision. Ideally, 'not sure' responses should be allowed initially, and then resolved by supplementary questioning.

The order in which publications occur in the interview may well have an effect on the readership estimates obtained. Employing a balanced set of different orders (randomly assigned to different interviews, of course) cannot eliminate the bias but may more evenly distribute it across different titles. However, if there is clear-cut evidence that one particular group of titles suffers disproportionately by being asked about last, there may be a good case for always taking it first, rather than relying completely on sub-randomisation. In any event, it is necessary to avoid publication orders in which respondents must plough through a morass of titles largely unfamiliar to them before they can reach ones on which they are more likely to be able to make a positive claim.

As regards the readership question itself, it is impossible to give unqualified endorsement to one of the alternatives rather than another, by reason of the balance of advantages and limitations outlined earlier. But if the Recent Reading road is taken, there is one further, hidden potential bias which can have material effects but which is avoidable, once recognised.

Let us suppose the critical question is, 'When did you last read or look at any copy of [title]?' and let us suppose further that, for convenience, one common set of answer categories is employed, applying equally to daily newspapers, weekly newspapers and magazines and to monthly publications: (1) 'yesterday'; (2) 'not yesterday, but within the last week'; (3) 'between a week and a month ago'; and (4) 'longer ago than a month'. For a daily newspaper, we shall then count into the 'Average Issue Readership' total only those who answer (1); for a weekly publication, (1) or (2); and for a monthly magazine, (1), (2) or (3).

Now consider a person unsure of the exact timing of their last reading occasion and who is therefore guessing, wholly or partly. If the answers of such readers are, consequently, distributed at random across the possible categories, the numerical chance of being classified as 'a reader' will be 1/4 for the daily newspaper, 2/4 for a publication appearing weekly and 3/4 for a monthly. These probabilities are clearly unequal and constitute a potential bias.

The actual occurrence of this phenomenon, in real life rather than merely in theory, is not difficult to demonstrate and quite dramatic shifts in readership estimates can be obtained merely by altering the ratio of the number of 'yes, reader' answer categories to the number of 'no, not reader' ones. Any possibility of bias from this source may be eliminated by equalising this ratio across publication groups, even if this entails using other than a common question for all titles. (The problem is not resolved merely by concealing the answer categories from the respondent.)

The last item in this short list of potential pitfalls concerns reading frequency. Again assuming a Recent Reading survey type, a long scale should not be used and, for sure, numerical claims about regularity of reading should not be accepted at their face value.

FUTURE OUTLOOK

Over the 50- or 60-year history of readership research that has elapsed to date, a very large corpus of empirical knowledge on the strengths and weaknesses of different research approaches has grown up, but the basic concepts have been few: the idea that total audience exceeded circulation, which spawned the Through-the-Book technique; the Recent Reading 'model' and its extension to take account of replicated and parallel reading; and the concepts of reading frequency and of probability of contact with the average issue.

The measurement methods which have developed around these concepts sometimes appear more radically different, the one from the other, than is the case in truth; thus, First Reading Yesterday is a 'natural' offspring of 'classic' Recent Reading, by virtue of the latter's well-acknowledged limitations as regards recall accuracy and model bias.

Whilst sage prognostications are just as likely to be proved wrong in this area of applied social science as anywhere else – particularly given the pace of technological change – it nonetheless seems unlikely that readership research's next 50 years will see the addition of startling new concepts, such as to change the underpinning of measurement methods. Rather, it seems likely that the ways in which already familiar data are captured and processed will be the locus of development.

Two requirements common to readership measurement and to many other areas of marketing research are the need, first, to capture a record of a certain piece of consumer behaviour – here, contact with a newspaper or magazine – and then to make those data machine-readable, so that they may be processed. In both these areas, the computer has made and is making a remarkable impact.

Computer Assisted Telephone Interviewing (CATI) removes from the interviewer any concern for question order, since the software guarantees that the correct wording appears on the screen in the right sequence, having regard not only to the basic questionnaire but also, at any particular point in the interview, to the pattern of the replies already given; and those replies are keyed direct to disk, allowing 'instant' editing and analysis, the moment an interview is completed. Such a system is very well suited to readership research (apart from the lack of visual prompting), given the complex rotations and routing in many questionnaires. Now, CATI advantages can be taken into the field, given the ever-increasing portability and ever-decreasing cost of laptop machines, with the consequent growth in Computer Assisted *Personal* Interviewing (CAPI).

Currently, CAPI-based readership interviews may still also employ printed materials, to some degree; but there is no reason why, for example, full-colour prompts should not be stored within the CAPI program and displayed to informants on the interviewer's screen.

We referred earlier to the possible use of videotext and teletext technologies for presenting a readership questionnaire (or an 'electronic diary) in a respondent's own home, on their TV set's screen or on a special terminal. Another possibility would harness the barcodes now printed on the covers or front pages of many (though not all) publications, which uniquely identify not only title but issue, too. We could equip a panel with light pens (to scan the relevant bar code whenever reading took place), with a solid-state storage device to hold the information thus captured (easily extended to date and time of reading) and with a means of downloading the data to a central computer, overnight, and so on.

In many areas of research, but particularly in relation to the mass media, the aim is to devise an objective, entirely 'passive' system of measurement, such that informants' voluntary co-operation does not have to be sought, nor is the researcher dependent on the veracity of the data they offer. For the measurement of television audiences, a number of such passive systems are under test (see Chapter 3): by various means, they 'sense' the presence of people in the viewing room and, hopefully, count and identify them.

For newspapers and magazines, the analogous aim would be to 'sense' the proximity of a person to a copy of a publication – and capture the title and issue concerned. Two systems have been proposed – and proved workable, in principle. Either would require the insertion, within the thickness of a page, of a micro-thin 'chip'; this insertion would have to apply to each and every copy of each and every issue of each and every title that was to be measured. The natural flexing of the pages that occurs when a publication is read would then generate either an ultrasonic signal, or a high-frequency radio one. The signal would be picked up and the 'reading' event logged by miniaturised receivers, carried by a panel of respondents, probably in the form of a wristwatch. The designs and the patents exist; all one needs is the funding.

FURTHER READING

The periodical literature relating to readership research is very extensive; an English-language-only bibliography would run to over 500 citations. However, many of these papers are too narrow and specialised for present purposes.

Without doubt, the best state-of-the-art overview is provided by the contributions to the six international symposia which have now been held. In four out of these six instances, complete proceedings have been published, all edited by Harry Henry. The full references are: *Readership Research: Theory and Practice. Proceedings of the First International Symposium New Orleans 1981*, London, Sigmatext, 1982 (out of print); *Readership Research: Montreal 1983. Proceedings of the Second International Symposium*, Amsterdam, Elsevier Science Publishers, 1984; *Readership Research: Theory and Practice.*

Proceedings of the Third International Symposium Salzburg 1985, Amsterdam, Elsevier Science Publishers, 1987; *Readership Research: Theory and Practice. Proceedings of the Fourth International Symposium Barcelona 1988*; London, Research Services Ltd/The British Market Research Bureau, 1989. A relatively short summary of these proceedings is available in the present author's *Dear Reader. Some Readership Measurement Questions ... and Some Answers*, distributed by Research Services Ltd, Research Services House, Elmgrove Road, Harrow, Middlesex HA1 2QG. There was no publication of the proceedings of the Fifth Symposium, held in Hong Kong in 1991. A nearly complete set of papers of the Sixth Symposium (San Francisco, 1992) may be available from Research Services Ltd but is likely to go rapidly out of print.

Chapters on print media research will also be found in the *Consumer Market Research Handbook* (third edition, 1986), edited by Robert M. Worcester and John Downham and published by McGraw-Hill, London, on behalf of the European Society for Opinion and Marketing Research (ESOMAR); and in *A Handbook of Market Research Techniques*, edited by Robin Birn, Paul Hague and Phyllis Vangelder and published in 1990 by Kogan Page, London. In the Marketing Research Monograph series there is *Print Media Research*, edited by Guy Consterdine (Amsterdam, ESOMAR, 1988), a collection of papers covering, *inter alia*, the Through-the-Book/Recent Reading controversy, readership panels and 'qualitative' measurements.

Two European viewpoints are offered in Eva-Maria Hess's *Leserschaftsforschung in Deutschland. Ziele, Methoden, Techniken*, published in 1981 by the market research department of Burda, Offenburg; and *Come misurare l'audience della stampa. Le ricerche di readership: problemi e metodi*, by Costantino Jannacone, published in 1990 by Lupetti & Co., Milan.

Paul Sumner has provided an invaluable guide to the computer's role in readership research and, particularly, to the mathematics of audience accumulation and schedule analysis; the text is totally accessible to the non-mathematician and covers much more of the readership waterfront than just the formulae. The title is *Readership Research and Computers*, published in 1985 by Newsweek International, London.

Readership Research and the Planning of Press Schedules, by Guy Consterdine (Aldershot, Gower, 1988) bridges the gap between the design of readership surveys and the application of their data. In the latter area, the classics (but covering all media, not just newspapers and magazines) are Simon Broadbent's *Spending Advertising Money*, (London, Business Books; first published 1970, but latterly revised) and *Media Planning* by James Adams, published in 1971 by Business Books on behalf of the Institute of Practitioners in Advertising.

Chapter 6

The audience to outdoor posters

Derek Bloom

Users of any advertising medium need to be able to select units – newspaper or magazine titles, television or radio spots, poster sites – in a logical fashion; they need to calculate what proportion of their target audience will be 'covered' by the resulting campaign, and with what frequency. There are, however, particular difficulties in providing this information for outdoor posters.

First, posters are pure medium. Apart from the paper on which they are printed and the physical structures that support them, they consist of nothing but advertising. They are not embedded in information or entertainment, though they may provide something of both, and are seldom consciously 'used', unlike newspapers and magazines, or radio and television programmes. Contact with them is quite unintentional – a casual and unremarked consequence of being in the streets on foot or in vehicles, in the tube and other public places. People can no more accurately recall how many posters they encountered last week than how many manhole covers they passed or how many doors painted green.

Second, the medium consists of huge numbers of individual panels delivering widely different sizes of audience. These audience sizes fluctuate from day to day around their own averages, which also change in the longer run. In Britain there are about 130,000 poster panels at 70,000 sites or locations, unevenly distributed about our towns, and probably no two are passed by exactly the same number of people in a week. In addition, there are over 400,000 panels of various sizes on or in buses, rail and tube trains and stations, collectively known as 'transport'. Audience research for the latter is mainly confined to the London Underground and London Transport buses; it is not considered here.

Third, merely passing a poster is not sufficient to define an audience contact; there has to be an opportunity to see it. Some posters are well positioned for visibility, others less so. A complete research system should encompass this factor.

Poster audience research systems differ widely from country to country. Some of these differences are detailed later. Factors that have contributed to this include the resources available and the way in which posters are bought and sold. In most countries, the medium attracts only a small share of advertising expenditure, out of which the poster 'contractors' have to find the money needed to fund research. (In the UK, posters account for 3.6 per cent of the total: two-thirds 'outdoor', one third transport.) Campaigns may be organised town by town, or on a regional or national basis. They may be *ad hoc* combinations of individual sites or they may consist of one or more preset 'packages'. It may be normal for campaigns to last just one or two weeks, for eight or more weeks – or even to be continuous.

It can also be said that there is a research tradition in a country that is likely to influence decisions about future investigations. There is a strong case for continuity in the interests of comparability, and users are most at home with the familiar.

COVER AND FREQUENCY SURVEYS

For planning purposes, a cover and frequency model is indispensable. This has to be based on information about the travel habits of a representative sample of inhabitants which is large enough to be analysed by demographic and geographic group. Typically, a survey is conducted in which respondents are asked to recall their journeys in the recent past, the period prescribed varying from country to country – yesterday, the last few days, the latest week – using some kind of prompt: maps or illustrations of places they might have passed. Alternatively, they might record journeys in diaries.

The first sample survey of this kind was carried out in Fort Wayne, Indiana, in 1946 and the first diary study in Cedar Rapids, Iowa, in 1949, both for the American (poster) Traffic Audit Bureau. In Fort Wayne respondents were interviewed at home about travel behaviour 'yesterday' only. It was found that 76.2 per cent of adults left their homes at some time in the day, and 60.2 per cent passed poster sites: on average 17.4 panels.

It appeared that men were more exposed to posters than women were, the young more so than the old, the employed more than the unemployed. These have turned out to be enduring and universal characteristics of the medium, reflecting the relative extent to which different groups move about the streets. Whereas 89.3 per cent of employed people in Fort Wayne left home yesterday, only 58.6 per cent of housewives did, and so on. The Cedar Rapids study showed that 80.7 per cent went out of doors daily, and in the course of 30 days 98.7 per cent went out at some time. Copland (1963: 68) recounts, 'Of the eight who did not go outdoors at all, three were permanent invalids, one was in hospital, and one was in jail the entire 30 days.'

For any combination of poster sites identified on the routes, these research results enabled the build-up of cover and frequency to be calculated. Although no attempt seems to have been made to generalise from the results of either of the early American studies, such findings lend themselves to being modelled in a robust and plausible way.

In this form of audience research the area investigated may be just the city of residence or it may be a larger territory, even the country as a whole. The longer the period the greater the strain on the memory, the larger the area the greater the strain on the technique. Do they recall exactly the route of an unimportant journey last Tuesday week? Do they recognise streets on a map or photographs of street scenes in a town hundreds of miles away that they visit very rarely?

It is also possible to use data deriving from claims about miles or hours travelled, by mode of transport, to model cover and frequency, but this does not enable the specific sites passed to be identified. It is a less accurate procedure, but it has the advantage of low cost. In practice only vehicular audiences have been treated in this way.

Whichever kind of travel information is used, 'grossing-up' cover and frequency calculations to the population represented by the sample will tend to understate the true weight of road traffic for various reasons. It is also the case that it will produce different results according to the size of the community under consideration. The smaller the community, the larger the proportion of those passing local poster sites who come from elsewhere.

THE COPLAND MODEL

In Britain during the immediately postwar years, posters were bought and sold on a town by town basis. Even the largest contractors did not have national holdings; rather they possessed strengths in particular regions and cities. Mills and Rockleys Ltd, a leading outdoor poster agency at the time, saw the need for a more scientific approach to planning the medium and therefore commissioned a series of research studies. The first of these was concerned with effectiveness; it demonstrated that recall varied in relation to size and length of campaign.

The second, under the direction of Brian Copland, bore more directly on the question of audience estimation. In-home surveys of travel over the previous week within each of nine towns and their immediate hinterlands were conducted between late October and mid-December 1952. Excluding their hinterlands, the towns ranged in population size from 17,000 to 308,000 for the administrative areas concerned.

Respondents were shown maps with the locations marked on them but were not told that these were poster sites. They were asked about each of their journeys the previous day, then about the day before, and so on back through the week. It was found that, across the nine towns, 94 per cent of adults left home at some time during the week.

All the posters in each town were identified, and where several were positioned at a single location they were treated as one site. Sixty was considered to constitute a practical limit to the number of sites that could reasonably be used for study in any one area, and where the total was larger a random sample was selected. Consequently the fraction of all sites involved varied by town from 8 per cent to 100 per cent.

Copland was well aware that audience size varied considerably from site to site, and that the visibility of posters displayed on them varied too, remarking,

> In order to find out whether members of the primary media audience will have 'a very good chance of seeing' it would be necessary to examine and classify every poster site according to the ease with which a passer-by could in fact see the poster. Unfortunately the characteristics of poster sites differ very greatly, and no sound basis has yet been discovered for evaluating the chance of seeing.

(Copland 1955: 15)

Randomly choosing 5, 10 and so on up to 50 of the sites used in each town, Copland calculated passages past them per head (1) amongst those who had passed at least one site, that is, the audience and (2) amongst all respondents. Clear patterns were revealed (Fig. 6.1 and 6.2). The slope of the graph lines depended on the size of the town: the smaller the town the steeper the slope, reflecting the fact that an individual has a greater chance of passing any one site in a small town than in a large one. The relationship was so regular that he was able to derive the rate of slope for any town simply from its population size. He called the resulting value A.

The point at which the audience line met the vertical axis varied slightly from town to town, but on average it was about 4, so Copland treated this as a constant, which he labelled B. If S is the number of sites used for a campaign in a town, AS is the weight of a town campaign expressed as passages per resident adult, so that B is the difference in average frequency between a member of the population and a member of the audience. Consequently, $AS + B$ represented the average frequency of a campaign of S sites amongst those covered, and cover as a decimal fraction was necessarily $AS/(AS + B)$. Applying this to specimen campaigns was shown to fit the facts to an acceptable degree of accuracy.

Copland's model was for campaigns, not individual sites, but if B really is a constant it should apply to a campaign of just one average site, or the equivalent in audience delivery of one such site, reducing frequency to $A + B$. The larger the town the smaller A becomes and the less important in $A + B$; for London A was later shown to be 0.0332. Implicitly, then, B approximates to the frequency with which the average site is passed by the average member of its audience – for brevity: 'site frequency'.

A has convenient properties. Multiplying it by the number of sites in a town tells us the total number of passages made there by the average adult resident in a week. Multiplying it by the adult population tells us the total number of passages delivered weekly to local adults by the average site in a town. It follows that, if passages per site can be discovered by some other means, the A value can be calculated, and Copland believed that traffic counts were an alternative to carrying out surveys for the purpose.

During the late 1970s the Copland model lost favour because it was not well adapted to the changing needs of campaign planning for the medium. An inability to provide A values for target groups was one source of discontent. There were others:

- Increasingly, advertisers planned their campaigns on the basis of television regions, generally in the form of the Incorporated Society of British Advertisers' non-overlap areas, and there was no method for calculating A values for these – nor a national A value.
- Most campaigns are for longer than one week. The industry adopted a rule of thumb that doubling the period was equivalent in its effect to doubling the weight in a one-week campaign, but this was arbitrary and implausible.
- Sites vary widely in their audience size, but Copland's assumption was that sites in any campaign were, on average, average. He made no allowance for visibility and its variation from panel to panel, treating a gross passage as an OTS.

The thrust of the poster campaign buying process was towards the

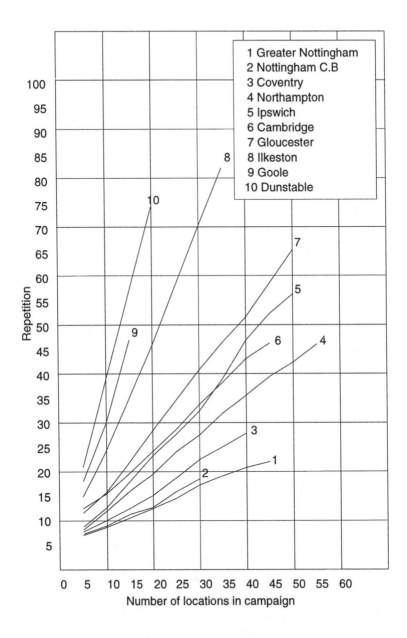

Figure 6.1 Passages per head amongst the audience

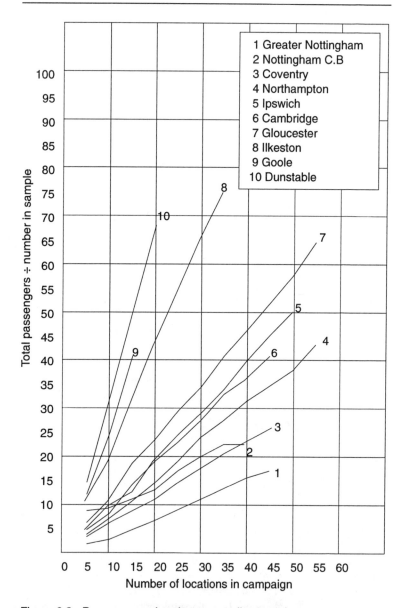

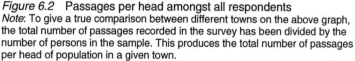

Figure 6.2   Passages per head amongst all respondents
Note: To give a true comparison between different towns on the above graph,
the total number of passages recorded in the survey has been divided by the
number of persons in the sample. This produces the total number of passages
per head of population in a given town.

selection of individual sites because of their alleged high audience, superior visibility or special position: 'line-by-line' rather than in 'packages' convenient to contractors. The trend increased after British Posters' joint sales organisation was proscribed as anti-competitive.

A turning point was reached during an industry conference in Nice in 1981, at which strong criticism was levelled at the contractors by representatives of advertising agencies over the lack of satisfactory audience research. They demanded information about the characteristics of every site, including an estimate of potential audience so as to make possible calculations about the audience delivery of any campaign. This was an extremely tall order, as it amounted to providing usable data for each minute fraction of a medium which itself accounted for under 3 per cent of advertising expenditure. Even so, the contractors agreed, and they set up a working party with representatives of the advertisers and of the advertising agencies.

OSCAR: OUTDOOR SITE CLASSIFICATION AND AUDIENCE RESEARCH

The working party recommended:

• a complete listing and classification of all relevant UK sites, including information about each individual panel situated there,
• a measure of visibility for individual panels,
• a model enabling estimates of vehicular and pedestrian audiences to be made for each location, on the basis of a carefully measured sample representative of the poster population across the country.

This was agreed by two newly formed organisations: the Outdoor Advertising Association (OAA), comprising all the main contracting companies and many smaller ones, and the Joint Industry Committee for Poster Audience Research (JICPAR), which included representatives of the media owners, the advertisers and the advertising agencies, as in all other JICs. It also included representation of the poster specialists who select sites and assemble 'line-by-line' campaigns for buyers. The research was entirely funded by the OAA. After a gestation period of four years, a system known by its acronym of OSCAR was launched in October 1985 and has since been improved in various ways. It combines a detailed census of roadside sites, together with other sites deemed to be 'outdoor' such as those in shopping centres and car parks, where the panels were controlled by companies belonging to the OAA, with a statistical model which estimates vehicular and pedestrian audience levels. The database also holds information on the characteristics of individual sites. Initially some sites in Northern Ireland were included, but for several years research information has related only to Great Britain.

The OSCAR model calculates the number of passages per week for each site on the basis of its characteristics, and this 'Gross Audience' is adjusted on the basis of an index of visibility relating to each panel at the site calculated from its scores on a number of criteria.

NOP Market Research Ltd were, and still are, responsible for collecting comprehensive information on each poster site and panel, amounting to 12 million bits of data, which they hold on computer file for the industry together with the estimation equations. Information can be extracted for individual sites or any combination of sites that might be of interest. Table 6.1 lists the information collected for every poster.

Table 6.1   Information collected for every poster site

- Site address
- Number of panels by size
- Name of contractor
- Site and panel references
- Town and district codes
- ISBA TV area
- Population and distance to next town
- Type of location: principal shopping, minor shopping, residential, commercial, and so on, distance from centre
- Road type: orbital, main, trunk, and so on
- Junction type, and vehicular and pedestrian entry points
- Traffic flow, traffic lanes, bus routes, traffic lights
- Proximity to retailers by type, pubs, offices, schools and special features, e.g. railway stations and sports grounds
- A two-minute count of passing vehicles

Additionally, fieldworkers had to draw a sketch map (Fig. 6.3) and assess the visibility of every panel. The entire process was so demanding that on average they completed only six sites per day. As the task amounted to a virtual census of poster sites in the country, it was a protracted one.

The model itself was created by Audits of Great Britain (AGB) on the basis of audience counts at a representative national sample of 437 sites in September 1983 after a pilot exercise using counts at a different sample of 150 sites the previous year. At the earlier stage it was found that the average number of occupants for vehicles of various types by time of day

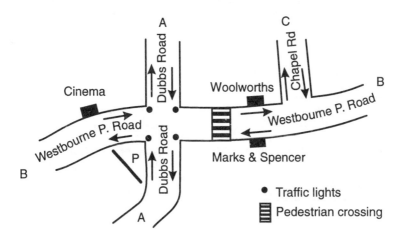

Figure 6.3 Sketch map of a poster site

and day of week could be predicted with great accuracy, so that in the main stage it was necessary only to count pedestrians and vehicles by type. The counting procedures were laid down in detail and their execution carefully controlled.

AGB statisticians analysed the relationships between the numbers of people passing on foot and in vehicles on the one hand, and the characteristics of the sites on the other (Table 6.2), using multiple regression techniques. They developed not one model but 11: vehicular audiences in conurbations versus other towns, pedestrian audiences in town centres versus other locations and, within these, different ones for weekdays, Saturdays and Sundays – but Sundays were the same for pedestrian audiences in both types of location. The estimates by day were aggregated to provide one-week estimates. In the vehicular case they were reduced by 10 per cent, one-tenth of a separate estimate based on the short counts being substituted, as this was found to improve accuracy. According to Bloom and Bowles:

> The degree to which the AGB model can accurately predict the audiences for sites can be evaluated, for the experimental sites, by comparing the consistency between audiences predicted by the model and those actually obtained from the counts. In statistical terms, this is done by examining how much of the variation between actual audience

Table 6.2   Key site characteristics for the OSCAR models, in order of importance

Vehicular audiences	Pedestrian audiences
• Town type	• Population
• Distance to next larger town	• Town type
• Distance to town centre	• Distance to next
• Location code	larger town
• Special features	• Shops nearby
• Junction type	• Location code
• Road classification	• Special features
• Number of traffic lanes	• Number of pedestrian
• Bus routes	entry points
• Traffic lights	• Estimate of
• Estimate of vehicular traffic	pedestrian traffic

levels is accounted for by the model. In the case of the pedestrian model, 88 per cent of all the variation between actual audience levels, for different sites, was explained ... In the case of the vehicle model, 87 per cent of the variation between actual audience levels was accounted for by the models.

No statistical model could be expected to predict the audience for any individual site with complete accuracy. The degree of accuracy in estimating audiences will, however, improve when groups of sites are considered rather than individual sites. In order to test the predictive power of the model, 100 random sub-samples of groups of ten sites were selected from the sample, and the model audience estimates compared with the actual traffic counts. The mean percentage error of prediction for these groups of sites never exceeded five per cent for vehicular audience estimates, nor 11 per cent for pedestrian audience estimates. These levels of accuracy improved slightly when larger groups of sites were considered.

(Bloom and Bowles, 1986: 234–5)

Sites in pedestrian-only areas such as shopping precincts, car parks and subways had markedly different characteristics from those on roads bearing vehicular traffic, but there were only 25 of them in the sample of sites at which full counts were made. While this was proportionate to their share of all sites in the country, it was a small number in absolute terms. Eventually it was decided to reclassify the entire population of such sites, and in 1987 audience counts were carried out at a fresh sub-sample of 100, the results being remodelled.

It does not matter how many people pass a site if none can see the posters displayed there and, while the wholly invisible poster may not exist, sightlines for many are badly obstructed and few are perfect in this respect. Taking the simple example of a T-junction (Fig. 6.4), the panel at P is parallel to traffic passing either way along road R, but seen only obliquely by them. It is head-on to the traffic moving into the junction along road Q, but invisible to traffic going in the opposite direction.

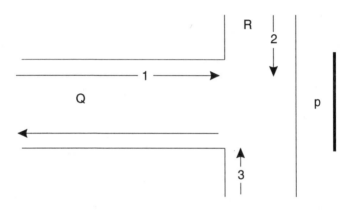

Figure 6.4   Poster visibility

On the basis of industry experience, a number of factors were identified and fieldworkers were required to assess them for each panel from the vantage point of every road from which it could be seen, up to a maximum of four roads (Table 6.3).

Table 6.3   Visibility factors in the OSCAR system

Vehicular visibility	*Pedestrian visibility*
• Distance at which visible	• Proportion able to
• Angle to road	see the panel, as
• Competition from other panels	judged by the
• Deflection from line of sight	fieldworker
• Degree of obstruction	• Competition from
• Height of panel from ground	other panels
• Illumination	• Illumination

The scores on each factor are combined according to an agreed formula to produce an index for pedestrian and another for vehicular visibility, each normally being less than 100 per cent. These indices are then applied to the gross passage figures to produce 'net' audience figures or opportunities to see (OTS). Across all panel sizes, on average the reduction from gross to net is about 70 per cent, suggesting that the visibility scoring system is quite severe. Differences between poster sizes are not fully reflected in the scores because the system was originally intended only to reflect variations in visibility within size.

The databank is continually updated for changes in the poster universe as sites are eliminated, new ones built, and old ones reconstructed. In addition 10 per cent of all existing sites are visited each year for reassessment.

OSCAR reports

Every six months an *OSCAR Digest* is published which gives a useful summary of the OAA poster universe. For Britain, for each ISBA region and for every local government district where there are posters, it provides:

- number of panels by size owned by each member company,
- audience scores – highest, lowest, average and most frequent scores for vehicular, pedestrian and combined audiences, for each poster size.

This standard report is not specific to campaigns, but it is useful both in planning and as a basis for comparison. Detailed data about each site and panel are held on computer file by NOP Posters, and every contractor holds his own information in one form or another. The 'working system' can be accessed to:

- establish the number of panels that have audiences over a given size or are in particular locations,
- generate lists of panels which conform to buying criteria such as proximity to a relevant type of retailer,
- give similar information for panels in a campaign together with their combined audience delivery.

Limitations of OSCAR

OSCAR provides media planners and buyers, and their clients, with an enormous amount of data on posters owned by members of the OAA, but there are contractors outside the association and some of them matter in certain parts of the country. There are constant changes in the poster universe, and classification of new sites is bound to trail the true situation to a small extent; it can never be quite up-to-date. A recent *OSCAR Digest* recorded an OAA poster universe of 108,700 panels, of which 103,100 had audience estimates.

A very heavy burden was and is placed on fieldworkers. Several of the questions are a matter of judgement rather than of readily determinable fact, so that two equally conscientious people could quite legitimately come to somewhat different conclusions about the same sites and panels.

In terms of the model itself, there are problems. First, audience estimates for individual panels must be less accurate than for sets of panels, and there is no way of determining by how much. On occasion an estimate will be wide of the mark. As the highly ambitious objective set at Nice was to deliver a reliable audience measure for every panel, this is unsettling to users in so far as they are aware of it.

Second, OSCAR estimates ultimately depend on traffic counts made in September 1983, and so cannot allow for seasonal variation. Gradual changes in the road network and in motoring habits will result in their being less accurate as time goes on, eventually making it necessary to recalibrate the model.

Third, the visibility system was based, not on fundamental research, but on the judgements of experienced people. This gives it a robust, commonsense, character but it has its shortcomings. For instance, angle means angle to the road rather than to the traffic; it classes panels as being parallel, angled or head-on rather than as somewhere along a continuum measured in degrees.

In spite of these qualifications, OSCAR was a huge step forward in providing a 'currency' that was relevant to the way in which the outdoor medium is organised, bought and sold today. Site selection has become more objective. Planners have a means of summing audience delivery across sites. Negotiators can calculate costs per thousand OTS. Owners have criteria by which to improve their holdings and in general the medium has become more accountable.

A NEW COVER AND FREQUENCY SYSTEM

OSCAR focuses on individual sites and panels. It estimates their audiences individually, but adding up those estimates for the panels constituting a campaign does not tell enough for effective media planning. There was a clear need for a cover and frequency system that meshed in with the new data: one that worked at national and regional levels, delivered estimates for target groups other than just adults, and did so for campaigns varying in duration as well as in weight. Above all, it should use OTS as input units rather than sites. OSCAR had shown that sites varied enormously in gross audience, and that allowing for visibility to arrive at OTS could make these differences even greater, so that treating campaigns simply as numbers of sites when calculating cover was bound to be extremely crude and, in many instances, misleading. Few advertisers set out to buy 'average' sites.

Copland's idea that traffic counts could be a route to the calculation of A values was not correct for individual towns unless the proportion coming from elsewhere was known, but at the national level there is no 'elsewhere' to worry about, with the exception of a relatively tiny number of overseas visitors who can safely be ignored. Consequently, a national A value can be obtained very simply. A single passage is made by one individual, and the probability that it is made by the average person in the population must be unity divided by the population of Great Britain: 55.2 million in 1986.

OTS are not different entities from passages, but passages weighted for probability of exposure, so that it is entirely legitimate to substitute them for passages in this calculation. One divided by 55.2 million is an inconvenient number; it is more usefully expressed per million OTS. On this basis A worked out as 0.0181. Therefore, a million OTS per week became the input unit of the system and was labelled M. Thus 21,540,000 OTS per week was 21.54M. On the simplifying assumption that young people under the age of 15 accounted for their population share of OTS – a conservative assumption since their share is almost certainly slightly lower – the all adult A value was 0.0181 as well.

To arrive at A values for target groups a national survey was needed, but it was quite impractical for interviewers to carry street maps for every town in the country. In the spring of 1987 Research Services Ltd (RSL) mounted a pilot survey in the South West television region on behalf of the OAA. This tested a new approach: the traditional street map method for the home area if it was urban, or the nearest town if rural, together with a specially constructed atlas of the region as a whole to help in obtaining detailed descriptions of journeys away from the home area, where stops were made, and the address of the destination (Cornish and Windle, 1988).

These longer journeys nearly always fell into one of two categories: very regular and therefore familiar, such as long-distance commuting to work by car, or very unusual and therefore memorable journeys undertaken for a special reason such as a visit to a friend in hospital or to look at an historic house. In either case, normally the route was readily recalled. The data recorded by the interviewer was interpreted in terms of passages by head office coders using master maps on which the sampled sites were marked, including the few that were in rural areas. In destination towns the range of probable routes was generally very limited so that the scope for error was small. RSL also investigated the validity of general claims about weekly hours spent travelling by mode of transport as a proxy for level of exposure to poster advertising, comparing them with information drawn from the detailed reconstruction of individual trips for each day back through the week. It was found that the correlation was weak overall, though better for car travel than for walking. People simply cannot make these estimates with great accuracy, and posters are not spread evenly around the country.

The national survey

The next step was the extremely laborious and expensive task of mapping poster sites across the whole of Great Britain, and transferring the information to paper maps. Different sampling fractions were used for the various sizes of panel, amounting to 6,002 sites overall: about a tenth of the total. The main survey investigated journeys over one week in October–November 1987 amongst a quota sample of 704 adults aged 15 and over in clusters of five per locality. Thus there were about 140 clusters of respondents whose passages past a widely dispersed sample of sites was being measured. Only about a third of the sites were passed at all and a quarter of respondents recorded no passages. The mean number of journeys per respondent in the week was 12.1 as against the 13.2 recorded by the National Travel Survey.

On a national basis there was no difficulty about calculating the number of passages per site by size, from which the number implied for the universe of poster sites could be estimated. In expanding this to an estimate for the population as a whole, it was assumed that the resulting figure would be lower than that deriving from OSCAR, even after allowing for juveniles, because:

- taxi-drivers, sales representatives and others who generate exceptionally large numbers of passages were under-represented in the sample,
- respondents tended to recall fewer journeys further back in the week: the all-week average was 20 per cent lower than 'yesterday', which itself might have been inflated by within-week 'telescoping'.

Between them, these two factors seem sufficient to explain the 29 per cent shortfall from what might have been expected from OSCAR.

From the survey, A values were calculated for a range of target groups at the national level, and each could be indexed on the all adult value as 100. Multiplying each indexed figure by 0.0181 in turn gave target group A values per million OTS. The all adult A value for each region was simply derived from its population in the same way as the national value. Allowing for differences in population profile, target group values were projected from national values and adjusted to fit the all adult values that applied. Plainly, it would have been better to calculate them directly from the survey, but sample sizes prohibited that.

The problem of 'elsewhere' reappeared with regional A values, though proportionally on a much smaller scale than for towns. Not surprisingly, a proportion of respondents in one region were found to have passed sites in another region – partly due to the accidents of sample geography (some clusters being close to regional boundaries) and partly due to longer journeys. Attempts to model this complicating factor were also defeated by the limitations of sample size. Consequently, what were referred to as 'import/export' passages (about 7 per cent of the total) were not treated separately so that, for instance, the OSCAR OTS in London that are caused by commuters from the Midlands or Anglia are implicitly attributed to Londoners. No provision was made for estimating audiences to campaigns within individual cities smaller than Greater London.

The average number of passages per respondent divided by the average number of sites passed per respondent was 4.1. This was seen as logically equivalent to B as earlier defined, and was rounded off to 4. Some variation by socio-demographic group was found, but it was not dramatic and could be explained as sampling error on the small numbers of respondents involved. As this was a one-week value, it was decided to establish empirically how it changed through time. It was obvious that a very high proportion of sites passed by the average respondent in Week 1 would also be passed by him or her in Week 2, and so on. However, there would be some journeys at least partly along new routes: ones that happened only every few weeks, were unique events, or were due to changed personal circumstances such as a new job.

A small study involving repeat interviews was conducted across four weeks and, of the 120 respondents recruited, 107 stayed the course. The results showed that B could be expressed as $2.84 + 1.16T$, where T was the number of weeks, so that its value was still 4 at one week but 5.16 at two, 6.32 at three, and so on. The Copland poster model was redefined as a function of the number of weeks, the A value and the number of million OTS per week, M, namely $TAM/(TAM + 1.16T + 2.84)$, which equals cover as a decimal fraction.

There are over 200 official A values nationally, including many for groups defined in terms of levels of exposure to other media, and a smaller number at the regional level, so that a wide range of poster planning needs are met. Besides the average frequency achieved amongst those covered by a campaign, it is also possible to calculate the percentage covered four or more times, ten or more times ... $N+$ times, and hence a complete frequency distribution can be obtained. An on-line system at NOP Posters can be accessed remotely using a PC equipped with a modem.

Various characteristics of the outdoor medium have emerged:

- the lower the initial cover, the greater the proportional gains from extra weight or length of campaign,
- increasing the weight or length of a campaign increases frequency proportionally more than cover, and therefore at the same cost per thousand, concentration of advertising effort into a short period maximises cover; while expending the same amount over a longer period achieves a higher frequency amongst those covered – as well as spreading impacts over time,
- rotating campaigns across geographically distinct sets of sites has the same effect of increasing cover at the expense of frequency, which is generally high relative to other media,
- the medium is shown to be particularly good at covering light TV viewers, for the obvious reason that they tend to move around the road system more than people in general.

The model implicitly assumes that the sites forming a campaign are spread fairly evenly over the population of the region or the country, which is not always the case in practice. The effect of greater concentration is to increase frequency at the expense of cover, but there is no way of estimating by how much. Also it has to treat all sizes alike, although they may vary to some extent in their audience profiles due to systematic differences in the locations where they are placed: main road junctions versus pedestrian precincts, and so on.

THE INTERNATIONAL PERSPECTIVE

Audience research methods vary between countries far more for posters than for any other medium. In Sweden they rely on respondent claims about numbers of sites passed made in a postal survey. In Australia an integral part of the system is the grading of sites by panels of taxi drivers. However, the main divide is the Atlantic, with quite different approaches adopted on opposite shores.

North America

Joint industry committees – the Canadian Outdoor Measurement Bureau (COMB) and, in the USA, the Traffic Audit Bureau for Media Measurement (TAB) – control very similar methodologies in their two countries in which the emphasis is on average vehicular traffic past sites for each 'market', that is, city or conurbation.

United States

In America TAB collects official road traffic counts from most city, county and state authorities, rechecking every few years. Where necessary these are supplemented by short counts made by the 'plant operators' (contractors) themselves, which can be verified by TAB. They are expanded by standard factors to one-day values which, in turn, are changed into 'daily effective circulation' (DEC) figures when adjustments are made for:

* direction of traffic,
* illumination to midnight or to dawn, so that they are for 12, 18 or 24 hours,
* number of adult (18+) occupants per vehicle. A recent study yielded an average of 1.35 occupants for the country as a whole.

For sales purposes figures are expressed in terms of 'showings' which are display weights expressed in terms of daily number of exposures related to the population of the market, so that a 100 showing would be 100 gross rating points per day. Standard quantities are showings at 25, 50, 75 and 100. Consequently, average audience estimates for an operator's plant suffice, though individual panel data is retained for site selection. Sales contracts are normally for 30 days.

The DEC concept incorporates a basic element of visibility in that only the traffic moving towards a structure is included. In addition, the industry has introduced an 'Outdoor Visibility Rating System' devised by the American Association of Advertising Agencies. Taking account of distance from the road, angle of panel, competition and visible approach time – at least five seconds at the maximum legal speed – interruptions to traffic and obstruction, OVRS rating points constitute a measure of quality, which may be helpful in selecting panels for a campaign, but do not affect DEC values.

Cover – 'reach' in America – and frequency are based on the answers to travel behaviour questions on two surveys: SMRB and MEDIAMARK, whose combined annual samples are 30,000. Both obtain estimates of urban miles driven in the past week and the past four weeks, respondents selecting from eight alternatives running from under 10 to over 250 miles per week. The link to poster advertising exposure was formerly made by means of annual 'Calibration Surveys' in a number of markets varied by size and region, rotated across the country over the years. The same questions as occurred in the SMRB survey were put to respondents; additionally they were asked to trace every trip made in the past week on a large scale street map, very much in the style of Copland, but one for each trip.

The industry has now dispensed with these research studies and transferred its statistical modelling to Harris/Donovan Systems of Toronto, who apply the same methodology in the USA that they have used in Canada with COMB data for some years. Pedestrian audiences are measured at bus shelters, but do not figure in the cover and frequency system.

Canada

Delcan, a traffic engineering firm, is contracted by COMB to provide the circulation figures, which are derived from the analysis of municipal and provincial traffic counts. For any site at which direct data are not available, Delcan makes a conservative estimate on the basis of nearby and analogous counts. On two-way roads, the vehicular count is halved. The system is used for all markets with a population in excess of 75,000 and for many between 25,000 and 75,000. There is an update programme, the frequency varying by size of market. For smaller communities, and to adjust for traffic changes between counts, reliance is placed on contractor statements, which are monitored by COMB. Counts are made of pedestrian audiences at transit (bus) shelters and in shopping malls.

A 'load factor' (occupancy factor) is applied to the vehicular count, and COMB further adjusts it according to the hours during which the poster panel is illuminated. Load factors vary by market from 1.3 to 1.8, partly in relation to average income per head. There is a separate Product Quality Rating system which embraces such considerations as positioning and obstruction, but this has no effect on audience estimates.

The medium is planned on a market by market basis, that is, city, town or group of towns – so a further adjustment is made to allow for the proportion of the traffic that originates elsewhere. As licence plate numbers indicate where vehicles are registered, it is fairly easy to estimate a factor for each market from sample checks. The out-of-market proportion has been found to range from 5 per cent up to 30 per cent and is represented as a bonus on top of the in-market Gross Rating Points (GRP) generated by a set of sites. One GRP is the number of in-market passages equal to 1 per cent of the population per market. Cover and frequency estimates are available for total population and 48 demographic groups: two sexes, eight age groups (12 to 17 being the youngest), three household income groups, and their combinations, but separately for vehicular and pedestrian audiences. Different empirical bases are used: one- and four-week driving patterns from an annual study by the Print Measurement Bureau (12,500 sample) and a survey by Canadian Facts of visitors to shopping malls by market. Audiences to transit shelter advertising are excluded from the cover and frequency system.

The vehicular model developed by Harris/Donovan Systems uses just one variable: claimed number of urban miles driven. For each demographic group this provides an exposure probability, which is assumed to be directly proportional to that number. Total outdoor impressions, after removal of the out-of-town element, can then be partitioned between the groups according to probability times number in the group. A binomial expansion of the probabilities is used to determine the percentage of each group covered by a campaign of a given weight, in terms of GRP, and the cumulative frequency and average frequency of exposure to it. An even distribution through the market area is assumed. The percentage claiming not to have driven at all in a month forms an upper bound to the potential cover in each group.

The relationship between claimed miles driven and exposure to the outdoor medium is an assumption which can be only broadly true, partly because posters are not evenly spread around urban areas, and partly because no adjustment is possible to allow for inter-respondent differences in the proportion of their car travel that is within the market analysed. If these differences are randomly distributed they do not matter, but if they have some systematic relationship to other group characteristics they will bias the results. In the USA no in-market adjustment is made, so there will be a pervasive upward bias to estimates, its significance varying by market.

Western Europe

Outside the British Isles, little attempt is made to measure the medium as input; a site is a site. In several countries, with varying degrees of success, output in terms of cover and frequency has been studied. In both France and Italy this has been on a town-by-town basis since campaigns are built up that way, with the inevitable consequences: failure to capture exposure to the medium away from the home area or to deliver true estimates for cover regionally or nationally.

Italy

Outdoor and transport have a 5 per cent share of total advertising expenditure, and sites are sold as packages. In 1981 a joint industry committee was established by the outdoor association together with the organisations representing advertisers and agencies. The outcome has been ICSA, a system of research, with DOXA and Remark as the research contractors. Its aims were:

- estimation of campaign cover and frequency in total and by demographic group, by studying the incidence of passages past sites in Italian cities and towns,
- assessment of the effectiveness of posters as an advertising medium. This aspect does not concern us here.

Later the same year an experimental study was conducted in Monza, a town of about 100,000 in the North West, testing a methodology which was subsequently applied in three further towns of similar size in different regions: Ferrara, Pisa and Lecce. In 1985 it was extended to Milan, a city of a million, and thereafter the results were modelled in relation to population so that cover and frequency calculations could be made for any weight of campaign in towns of all sizes.

The survey in Milan involved a sample of 2,000 adults, aged 15 and over, and aimed to measure their 'potential' OTS, that is, gross passages, and also their 'probable' OTS – in principle somewhat more reliable than visibility-adjusted passages. The first step was a census of qualifying structures amounting to 13,395 panels at 6,756 sites, classified by eleven combinations of size and type. Their exact positions were marked on maps and the co-ordinates read off with a digitiser into computer file.

Most respondents were asked only about their movements in the past two days (interviews on Wednesday to Saturday) or three days (interviews on Monday and Tuesday). A sub-sample of 100 agreed to be interviewed about their journeys round Milan over two weeks; this involved four interviews at intervals of three or four days. All journeys for each day were reconstructed in detail and mapped, each change of transport mode counting as a separate journey.

Interviewers had a sample of the sites marked on their maps and every time a passage was indicated they showed respondents two photographs of the site in question and asked, 'Did you glance in this direction?' Both 'potential' and 'probable' OTS were recorded and later keyed into the computer. It may be wondered how accurately respondents could recall whether or not they had looked in particular directions at large numbers of locations on specific occasions.

By taking successive samples of sites of a given number drawn at random, it was possible to arrive at predictions for cover and frequency for various campaign weights directly over one and two days. Extrapolations to fourteen days were made on the basis of the time effects observed amongst the subsample. Plausible relationships between socio-demographic group and exposure level were observed (Crisci, 1992).

France

In France, posters are sold in packages measured in terms of 'force', that is, the number of daily passages equivalent to the population of the town, very much as in America, but generally for only one week. With 12 per cent of a major advertising market, the medium has large resources at its disposal. Avenir, a leading French outdoor contractor, developed a technically sophisticated system for displaying town-by-town campaign information on screen, visually combining site and audience data. A street map of each town, including the position of every panel and the traffic flows that can see it, is held on computer file. The results of town-specific movement surveys are integrated with these and can be manipulated to provide cover and frequency estimates for any set of sites against any audience. Known as MAUD, it is an example of a 'Geographic Information System' or GIS.

Together with competitors Giraudy and Dauphin, Avenir financed a series of surveys with sample sizes varying by importance of town: 3,000 in Paris, 1,500 for urban areas over 900,000 population, 1,000 for those over 200,000, and 600 if over 100,000. It should be noted that only 50 per cent of the French population live in towns of 100,000 or above, but those account for 80 per cent of poster sites.

The sample in any town was divided into seven, two-sevenths being interviewed on Monday and one-seventh each day from Tuesday to Saturday. Each respondent, interviewed at home, was asked only about their movements the previous day (or over the weekend). Consequently, for towns with under 200,000 inhabitants, effective sample sizes were very small: equivalent to 110 for a whole week. Even the Paris sample was only equivalent to 550 for a full week. With the help of the interviewer, each journey was plotted on a separate town map, and it seems that they averaged 3.2 journeys per interview. Given the weekend weighting, that implies about 2.5 per day.

Passages were deduced from coincidences or near coincidences of grid references between movements and poster sites. Very few panels are sited parallel to the road, and therefore it was assumed that only persons moving towards a panel were a potential audience for it. Otherwise there was no visibility element in the calculation of audience size – not even illumination. For such short recall periods, problems of memory are minimal and the modest burden on the respondent makes for good co-operation, but modelling the results is dependent on conclusions about the relationship of one-week cover to one-day cover drawn from earlier studies. There was no direct measure of day-to-day site repetition, and it would have been misleading to fuse the Monday behaviour of X with the Tuesday behaviour of Y.

From 1983 to 1988 CESP carried out five similar studies on behalf of the industry as a whole, giving the results a more mathematical treatment. In 1989 these, together with results from two of the proprietary studies, were examined afresh. A strong relationship was discovered between size of population and E, 'passages per day per site per average adult resident': in effect, Copland's A value divided by seven. CESP also developed a model for cover, somewhat more complex than Copland's, but broadly similar in form.

This points up an insoluble problem: no population-based formula will be absolutely correct for all towns because it reflects a general relationship which does not allow for local differences in site quality. On the other hand, empirical town-by-town figures are only as good as the individual survey. These are expensive to conduct in the first place, let alone repeat to reflect changes in local journey patterns, and therefore are difficult to afford for every town of interest.

The Netherlands

About 10 per cent of advertising expenditure is on outdoor and transport. In 1988 SUMMO, in co-operation with the outdoor advertising companies and AGB Media, examined ways of measuring poster audiences which would allow for the structural characteristics of the medium in Holland. A high proportion of the Dutch population lives in an almost continuous urban belt stretching from Amsterdam to Rotterdam, with much daily movement from one part of it to another, so that a town-by-town approach was clearly inappropriate. While there are many packages, panels are also selected individually and assembled into 'custom-built' campaigns.

Consequently the analysis system had to be capable of calculating audiences for an almost infinite number of combinations of poster sites.

In 1990–1 a national research programme was carried out. This entailed:

- The identification of 17,000 poster panels, recording their salient characteristics, and mapping them.
- On a similar set of maps the routes were entered for all journeys made by a sample of 10,000 individuals over the age of 13 in the course of seven days.
- The time, main means of transport, and reason for each journey were recorded.
- Site contact probabilities per individual were established by comparing the two sets of spatial information above.

Contact probability was defined as 'actual presence in the street' close to a poster site without reference to the general visibility of the panel or the direction in which the respondent claimed to be looking when in the vicinity. Only 50 per cent of bus shelters were visited, together with all larger types of panel: a near census. Each was given a unique AGB code number.

Fieldwork was conducted in the autumn of 1990 and spring of 1991. Respondents were equipped with:

- a diary to record addresses, routes, day-parts, means of transport, and so on,
- street maps of the home city and of other cities identified at the recruitment stage as ones that they visited for work, shopping, social life, and so on,
- regional route maps,
- access to a help desk which could provide extra maps.

Of those recruited 77 per cent completed the task. As might have been expected, bus-drivers and other professional road users were under-represented. There was some evidence of respondent fatigue.

All but a handful of panels were passed by at least one respondent. Using the enormous database, for any combination of panels and any of a useful range of target groups, it was possible to examine the number of contacts, and the cover and frequency achieved nationally. For the larger target groups, this could also be done within any one of the five Nielsen regions, but not at the town level. No modelling was involved, except for attribution of audiences to the 50 per cent of bus stops not mapped.

Poster campaigns in the Netherlands are of one, two or four weeks' duration, and modelling was required to make audience estimates over the longer periods. Cover can be expressed as 100 per cent minus those not covered: [1–(1–C)]. For each day from Saturday to Friday, cumulative values for (1–C) were regressed against the number of days, both in logs. The fit was almost perfect and extrapolations not only looked plausible but also corresponded very closely with the findings from a multi-week study that had been carried out by another company. This approach was adopted, and it was found sufficient to take values for Day 1 and Day 7 from the database for projection.

On the reasonable assumption that the journey patterns of the population as a whole are not likely to change very much over two or three years, whatever may be the case for particular individuals, updating is a matter of mapping new sites and erasing demolished ones. However, even that is a considerable task using the current method, particularly as the intention is to do so four times a year. A less labour-intensive technique is needed for the updates, and even more so for any successor survey in a few years' time. The possibility of developing a geographic information system in which all the data would be held in digital form is under investigation. (Van Meeren, 1992)

Ireland

Advertising expenditure in the Republic of Ireland is low even for its small population, and the funds available for audience research are therefore limited, particularly for a medium with only 7 per cent of the total. There are c. 6,000 panels at outdoor sites, 'line-by-line' buying is prevalent, and contracts are normally for four weeks.

ORAC – originally the Outdoor Research Action Committee, but now Outdoor Research and Classification – established a database comprising all roadside sites, which were classified according to town size, neighbourhood and road type. For all panels displayed, visibility factors were assessed and converted into visibility scores to modify vehicular passage data.

Annual Average Daily Traffic figures were obtained from An Foras Forbatha Teoranta, the national planning institute, and from local authorities. If no official figure was available for a counting point sufficiently close to a site to plausibly represent it, a hand-count was made and grossed up using An Foras expansion factors. Daily figures were turned into monthly ones and multiplied by an occupancy figure of 1.8.

Having input data for vehicular audiences, the decision was made to add output data, so a cover and frequency survey was commissioned. With a respondent sample of 800 adults 15 years and over, the survey took place in October 1991 using methodology very like that in Britain. However, whereas in Britain each regular journey was tracked only once on the assumption that the route would not differ appreciably from occasion to occasion, in Ireland the process was repeated for each occasion that the journey had been made, revealing considerable variation in route.

Other major differences were that all sites except those at pedestrian-only locations were included, and that the way in which they were related to journey paths was by means of post-coding, that is, they were not marked on the maps used by interviewers, only on those used in the office. The term 'site' is inexact, each contractor having his own conventions, so that one might give a different site number to each panel at a single location while another might give the same number to a series of panels on structures strung out along a road. It was agreed that the determining factor was the location, with a distance of 50 yards between panels as the criterion of separateness.

The survey collected pedestrian as well as vehicular passages so that there was a need for pedestrian audience input data for each site. Counts were taken over a week at sites representing each of six types of location, and the results expressed as ratios to vehicular traffic. Since every site had been classified, each could be assigned to one or other type and an approximate weekly audience figure ascribed to it.

The survey yielded a vast amount of data despite the small respondent sample because of the near 'census' of sites. Ten sets of sites were drawn randomly at each of seven weights from 25 to 500 sites, and the cover and frequency attained for adults and for a range of target groups examined in relation to the input levels of these hypothetical campaigns. This was a more satisfactory basis for analysis than had been available in Britain. Regressing cover against AM (passages per person) in logs produced a series of models of the form $C = (AM)^V/B$, one for each of 66 target groups. Here B was 10^K, with K the constant in the logarithmic equation. Many V and B values were similar, so that A was the main discriminator. In order to estimate the cover delivered by multi-week campaigns, the Dutch example was followed: day-by-day cumulative cover figures for the hypothetical campaigns were extrapolated, but the results were then modelled for operational use.

FUTURE DEVELOPMENTS

It has been seen that in North America surveys no longer play a part in poster research except for the provision of claims about miles driven with which to apportion campaign exposures amongst car-borne travellers. On the continent of Europe, by contrast, the measurement of traffic past poster sites is dependent on respondent claims about their journey patterns, over a day or a week, using various elicitation techniques.

It seems clear that hybrid systems, as in Britain and Ireland, are to be preferred wherever line-by-line buying is the norm, despite the inevitable problems of reconciling sets of data collected by entirely different means. It would be realistic to recognise that levels of accuracy may have to vary with the importance of the different elements and the limitations of the methods available, and to accept that secondary use of others' data and facilities will be necessary if the system is to be affordable in the long run.

Geographic information systems

The cost of OSCAR, the input half of the British system, was so enormous in relation to the poster industry's limited means, that it is unlikely that the OAA would countenance expenditure on a comparable scale in future, although the need to update or replace it has been recognised. It is probable that the key to progress lies in the spatially dispersed nature of the medium, building the audience system into a geographic information system (GIS), that is, a computer-based combination of textual and numerical data with digitised maps. These comprise many layers of information: addresses, street centre lines, class of road, or whatever else may be relevant – such as underground pipes for a utility, or weights of traffic for a transport authority. The spatial relationships of any object identified, or inserted, to any other object can be calculated from their co-ordinates: distance or direction of x from y; the number of z within 100 metres or kilometres of x, and so on.

While great progress has been made with some applications, so far GIS has not realised its full potential in the UK despite the increasing power and scope of the software and the rapidly falling cost of computing. In part this is because of the pricing policy of the Ordnance Survey which licenses the use of the underlying maps. It may be that the way ahead lies in co-operation with some other organisation – a utility, a GIS supplier or the Ordnance Survey itself – which might allow carefully circumscribed use of their system for the purposes required by the poster industry at acceptable cost. However, NOP and some poster specialists have begun using GIS, albeit with maps of fairly small scale, poster positions being defined by their post codes, which locate them within a 100 metre square.

It would be preferable to capture the exact positions of all OAA sites. Handheld devices now exist which would facilitate the work. Once assembled, this geographical description of the medium would help in the selection of sites, including whether they fitted into non-standard areas such as client sales districts, as well as providing the framework for the audience system. Proximity data has been found to be useful in its own right, but some of it ages rapidly – types of retailer nearby, for example. As far as possible and affordable, proximity data of direct commercial value to advertisers, or for modelling purposes, should be sourced from the computer data bases now available. For the most part, this would be more accurate as well as more comprehensive than similar data collected by fieldworkers.

Better site-audience estimates

Within OSCAR 80 per cent of the gross audience and 72 per cent of the net is vehicular, so it is obvious where improvements would have the greatest effect on the whole. Most local authorities now use induction loops to monitor traffic at key points instead of the less-reliable pressure tubes, although those – and human enumerators – are still important for one-off counts. The Department of Transport has its own traffic data, analysed by type of vehicle passing 12,000 points around the country, on motorways and in towns.

It is probable that many authorities would be prepared to supply data at acceptable cost. Substituting reliable counts of vehicular traffic for model-derived estimates where counting points were very close to some sites would be a first step. From these and other data such as population, road class, street pattern and proximity data, better modelling of major sites could be achieved which allowed for regional and seasonal differences that do not figure in the existing OSCAR models.

Good data from these sources would be less abundant for lesser sites, and would have to be supplemented by short-term hand counts grossed up to one-week estimates unless affordable automated methods became available. Recent developments in neural network computing applied to video recordings look promising. Modelling the figures for major sites in the same city with the help of correlate data could be expected to produce realistic estimates.

Pedestrian flow-count figures for shopping centres can be bought quite cheaply from commercial sources, and again could be modelled. For sites in other locations, rather blander averages deriving from cover and frequency surveys might have to suffice. However, it is quite possible that neural network technology will be used here, eventually, as well.

Visibility

Real progress in this important aspect depends on a readiness to carry out fundamental research into the ability of pedestrians, drivers and passengers to see designs on poster panels, taking into account such considerations as weight and speed of traffic in addition to distance, illumination, competition and angle to traffic. It should be recognised that the apparent angle of a panel is influenced by its degree of setback from the road and by the width of the road, and that it changes as a viewer moves towards it.

Starting with simple experiments which themselves would reveal a good deal more than is known with any certainty at present, a not very expensive programme of research would enable an objective and practical visibility system to be developed which used database information, including position, angle and height from the ground as collected initially. Illumination could be given a different value according to season of the year. The aim with the visibility system, as with the gross audience models, would be to minimise fieldwork so as to reduce expense and scope for error.

Cover and frequency

There is no alternative to using survey methods, and any advance on the existing system would require larger samples. In-car navigation systems hold out the prospect of very accurate tracking of routes taken by drivers, which could reduce the interview load on respondents. Routes would be input to the GIS without any further site mapping, all poster locations being there already – a fact that itself ensured that there would be ten times as many passages per respondent journey day as in the 1987 study. The examination of hypothetical campaigns of different weights and types would be a practical proposition, as it was not after the existing British survey because of the varying fractions of site sizes used in relation to the small respondent sample.

As suggested earlier, the results for pedestrians could furnish average site audiences by type for lesser sites. Given local boosts to samples, audiences to transport media could be integrated into the system, and within-town audiences to outdoor could be modelled as well as regional and national audiences. The formulaic approach could be made more realistic and flexible and, with the accumulation of results from succeeding waves of research over time, eventually be replaced by simulation. At some point, a large-scale multi-week study would be needed.

REFERENCES

Bloom, D. and Bowles, T (1988) 'OSCAR: The Great Outdoors', in *New Developments in Media Research*, ESOMAR Seminar, Helsinki.

Copland, B. (1955) *The Size and Nature of the Poster Audience, Study* II, London, Mills & Rockley.

Copland, B. (1963) *A Review of Poster Research*, London, Business Publications.

Cornish, P. and Windle, R. (1988) 'Characteristics of the Poster Audience in Great Britain', in *Media and Media Research: How Far Can We Go?* ESOMAR Seminar, Madrid.

Crisci, M. T. (1992) 'Poster Research: From Cover and Frequency to Effectiveness', ESOMAR Seminar, Madrid.

Van Meeren, L. (1992) 'Outdoor Advertising Audience Measurement, the Dutch Solution', in *Media Research Meets the Future*, ESOMAR Seminar, Lisbon.

Chapter 7

Measuring cinema audiences

Richard Chilton and Paul Butler

Interest in measuring the audiences for cinemas comes from a number of industry sectors:

- Cinema advertising contractors, together with their clients and advertising agencies. Cinema advertising time can be sold only if a comprehensive description of the audience is provided.
- Cinema exhibitors. They have their own admission statistics, but they are also interested to know their share of the market, the composition of the audience and how particular films are doing. They also study very closely the potential location of cinemas.
- Cinema distributors. When planning the launch of a new film it is very helpful to study the audience from previous similar films. They are also keen to monitor through film tracking the progress of a new film as the publicity builds up.
- Video distributors. Many of the most successful video films were also successful in the cinema. Video film distributors are keen to study the success of cinema films as a guide to the video launch.

The basic measurements taken include:

- Cinema admissions. For reasons we will explain later it is necessary to collect admission figures weekly in support of cinema advertising.
- Audience composition. This tells us on average who is going to the cinema, for example, which age and social class groups.
- Audience by film. The audience composition for different films varies greatly and this needs to be plotted.
- Qualitative studies. Recall surveys can measure the impact of cinema advertising, appreciation of advertisements and so on.
- Film tracking. This is a weekly service for film distributors which, for example, plots the awareness of new films or the desire to see.

- Analysis of drive time. Cinema exhibitors plot the hinterlands of a potential new cinema to examine the possible audience.

THE REVIVAL OF THE CINEMA MEDIUM

Since its emergence as a commercial medium at the turn of the century, cinema has captured the hearts of millions. From the days of silent film through to today's advanced production and exhibition techniques the opportunities of reaching the public with a unique medium have been realised.

The late 1940s saw cinema as the social occasion of the week, providing relatively inexpensive entertainment for all. In the 1950s the grip of television began to take hold, potential audiences remained at home and screens closed.

Since the mid-1980s, however, cinema has enjoyed a sustained revival in popularity, despite the growth in home video. The year 1991 saw admissions climb for the seventh successive year, fuelled by quality film products and an unprecedented level of investment in new and refurbished cinemas. Probably the most significant change in the last few years has been the growth in purpose-built multiplex sites, which offer up to fourteen different screens, comfortable seating, quality sound and projection, food, drink and parking. Multiplexes are essentially multi-entertainment centres. The first opened in 1985; by the end of 1991 approximately a quarter of all UK screens were sited in such centres. The transition in the last 10 years is illustrated in Figure 7.1.

The revival in audiences and efficient marketing by the two advertising contractors, RSA Advertising and Pearl & Dean, has done much to boost cinema advertising revenue. Across 1989 and 1990, Advertising Association estimates show the growth in cinema revenue to outstrip any other form of display medium, increasing from £35 million to £39 million, an increase of 11 per cent. Cinema offers advertisers impactful delivery to a young audience with high disposable income and often difficult to reach via other media.

MEASURING CINEMA ADMISSIONS

Just as television has ratings and press has circulation for measurement of audiences, the cinema medium also has its own unique form of audience measurement. In some ways it is in a fortunate position in so far as measuring attendances is easier than monitoring exposure to television or

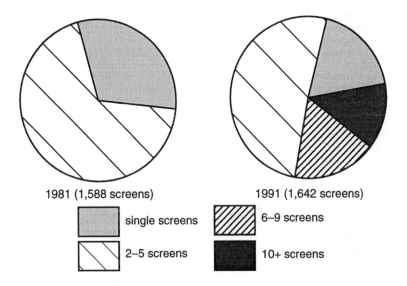

1981 (1,588 screens)   1991 (1,642 screens)

■ single screens   ▨ 6–9 screens

□ 2–5 screens   ■ 10+ screens

Figure 7.1   The development of multi-screen cinemas, 1981–91

radio. People actively choose to visit the cinema, purchasing a ticket for entry.

The most accurate, comprehensive and widely used source of UK admissions data is that commissioned by the Cinema Advertising Association (CAA). This provides weekly estimates of the total number of audience admissions to all circuit and independent screens that carry advertising. It is important that admission data be available on a regular basis with quick reporting of results. The CAA Monitor was established in 1984 and since 1989 it has been conducted by Gallup (Gallup, 1990a); figures before this date were supplied by Marplan.

Research method

Admission information is collected by telephone directly from the cinema operators. Circuit cinemas, accounting for about 70 per cent of all screens, are telephoned on a weekly basis. Usually one telephone call is made to a head office contact from each operator to collect admissions from all screens. The major circuits covered are shown in Table 7.1.

Table 7.1   Major circuits covered by the CAA Monitor

Apollo
Associated Tower
Cannon/MGM
Caledonian
CIC/UCI
Curzon
Jack Edge
Kingsway
Odeon
Showcase
UCI
Warner

With all circuits providing data on a weekly basis, the Monitor is based on a census of cinemas that govern about 80 per cent of all UK admissions. Admissions to the remaining 20 per cent of the market (the independent screens) are estimated using a representative panel. There are approximately 550 independent screens open in the UK, of which about 120 are included on the panel.

Panel cinemas are selected for each advertising contractor to be representative by ISBA area and number of screens within the cinema. Every quarter the panel of independent screens is checked to ensure representativeness with the universe of independent screens open. Each advertising contractor has access to confidentially supplied year-by-year admission information for screens to which they sell advertising space. The checks ensure that the average admissions for panel cinemas fall within plus or minus 10 per cent of average admissions for the universe of independent screens. Should the average fall outside the 10 per cent acceptability threshold then replacements are made on the panel (within the ISBA and screens per site guidelines outlined above). The CAA releases weekly admissions on a monthly basis, usually three to four weeks after the end of the calendar month.

Influences on cinema admissions

Since 1985 the cinema has been enjoying a marked revival; investment in new cinemas and continued quality popular appeal film product has done much to attract audiences. Figure 7.2 illustrates annual audiences to all cinemas accepting advertising over the period 1980–91. Admission levels fluctuate substantially throughout the year, as the analysis of weekly admissions throughout 1991 illustrates (Fig. 7.3).

Cinema-going is essentially a leisure activity, and participation is influenced by many diverse factors. The effects of some of these factors are considered below:

- Film product. The effect of the release of *Ghost*, the top box-office film of 1990, on admissions can be seen clearly in Table 7.2.

Table 7.2   Weekly admissions (in millions)

	1989	1990	1991
September	1.58	1.45	1.49
	1.78	1.35	1.58
	1.53	1.49	1.42
	1.52	1.43	1.47
October	1.47	2.01*	1.32
	1.64	2.21*	1.35
	2.08	2.98*	1.92
	1.72	2.49*	1.91

* *Ghost* on release

- School holidays. Children's film product is deliberately targeted for release around the key school holiday periods when the audience potential is maximised. Looking at weekly admissions throughout 1991 (Fig. 7.3), the effect of half-term breaks and full holidays can easily be identified.
- Television programming. Throughout the 1980s, cinema survived the growth of in-home entertainment very well. Research has shown that the growth of video, for example, has actually added fuel to the revival of the cinema, both benefitting from cross-promotion; similar effects are likely with the rise in popularity of film channels via cable or satellite. The quality of terrestrial programming can also have an effect on admission levels, for example major televised sporting events appealing to the core audience group (16–34 males) such as the Olympics and the World Cup can keep audiences at home.
- Weather and seasonal variations. The weather can affect the seasonal nature of the cinema audience. Sunny warm evenings in summer and very cold or wet evenings in winter can both depress cinema audience levels.

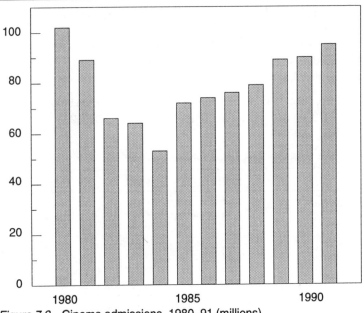

Figure 7.2   Cinema admissions, 1980–91 (millions)
Sources: DTI/Marplan/Gallup

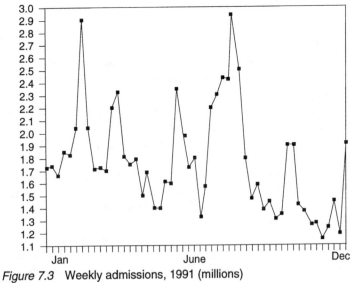

Figure 7.3   Weekly admissions, 1991 (millions)
Source: Gallup

Limitations of admission measurement

A major limitation is the non-inclusion of screens not accepting advertising. The film industry makes estimates of the complete market incorporating estimates of the few screens (approximately 120 of a total of 1,760) outside the CAA. It was estimated that non-advertising screens added about 8 million to the CAA recorded 93 million, giving a total industry of 101 million admissions in 1991. Since 1992, however, the Showcase circuit is accepting advertising. This means that the CAA Monitor will become more comprehensive.

AUDIENCE COMPOSITION

The admission statistics tell us how many people are going to the cinema, but they do not tell us who is going, that is, the characteristics of the audience. For this further information we must turn initially to two large continuous surveys – the National Readership Survey (NRS) (see Chapter 5) and the Target Group Index (TGI) (see Kent, 1993). These are very large surveys with current annual samples of 28,500 and 25,000 among adults aged 15–plus respectively. The large sample of the NRS is very convenient when it comes to detailed analysis such as breakdowns by area; the TGI is also very useful because of the information on product purchasing collected from the same respondents.

Both surveys have three questions on cinema-going. First, on frequency, 'How often these days do you go to the cinema?'; second, on recency, 'How long ago was the last occasion you went to the cinema?'; and third, on individual films. The first two questions form the basis of the CAA coverage and frequency model. The first question breaks the population into frequency cells, as can be seen in Table 7.3. This also provides an estimate of the number of visits per year of the adults in each frequency cell; for example, those in the one a month cell are reckoned to go on average 6.1 times a year. The total adult visits per year can also be estimated.

The calculation of the average annual visits is undertaken in two stages:

1   For each frequency cell we find out the proportion going to the cinema in the last week. This is the net weekly reach and using the binomial theory we can derive the probability of going to the cinema in an average half week. We use the half week since it allows for members of the public who go to the cinema twice a week. The average annual visits represent the half week probabilities multiplied by 104 (i. e. 52 X 2).

Table 7.3 Frequency of cinema-going

Frequency	Population	Half-week probability (× 1,000)	Average annual visits	Total visits (000s)
Once a week	561	360	37.5	21,015
2–3 times a month	1,554	119	12.4	19,270
Once a month	2,621	58	6.1	15,903
Once in 2–3 months	3,625	29	3.0	10,997
2–3 times a year	5,114	14	1.5	7,433
Less often	4,875	9	0.9	4,439
Never	26,850	NIL	NIL	NIL
Total	45,200		1.7	79,057

Source: CAA/NRS, 1991

2 There is a danger, however, that the total annual admissions may disagree with the admissions Monitor, and a weighting factor is applied to all the probabilities to bring the model data into line with reality. The Table illustrated is the weighted version. The probabilities are also weighted by ISBA area to fall into line with CAA admission estimates by region.

The method is very similar to that used to evaluate the exposure to press publications (average issue readership – see Chapter 5). Armed with the probabilities, we can produce the gross and the net coverage (by frequency cell) for any given number of weeks of cinema-going. When summed over all cells the gross cover (as measured by total admissions) divided by the net cover (the number of people going at least once) gives the average frequency of exposure.

This technique can be applied to any subgroup of the population with a reasonable sample size, for example, those aged 15–24. First we divide the subgroup up by frequency cells. Then we calculate half week probabilities by the method described above. This results in an estimate of annual admissions for that age group. If we do this for all age groups we end up with the audience profile by age. The audience composition in 1991 was as in Table 7.4.

From the CAVIAR survey (see below) we can look at the number of visits in the two months previous to the survey, again analysed by age (see Fig. 7.4). Children under 15 cannot be ignored. In the CAVIAR 9 survey they accounted for 14 per cent of all recent visits. The peak age for cinema

Table 7.4   Audience composition for 1991

	Percentage of average audience	Percentage of population
Male	51	48
Female	49	52
Age		
15–17	15	5
18–24	40	13
25–34	26	19
35+	19	63
Social class		
AB	26	18
C1	32	24
C2	22	27
DE	20	31

Source: CAA/NRS, 1991

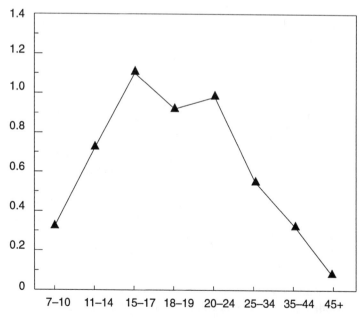

Figure 7.4   Average visits in the last two months by age
Source: CAVIAR 9 Survey

going is 15–17 and after the age of 24 there is for most people a steady decline in the cinema-going habit!

AUDIENCE BY FILM

CAVIAR (Cinema and Video Industry Audience Research) is sponsored by the CAA and supported by advertising agencies, cinema exhibitors, film distributors, video distributors and video retailers. In its present form this project is now in its tenth year. The questionnaire covers cinema, video films, television, satellite and cable, and newspaper and magazine reading (CAVIAR, 1991(a), 1991(b), 1991(c); ITT, 1991). We will concentrate here on the cinema side and consider first why the CAVIAR consortium members thought it necessary to supplement the information from the general questions in the National Readership and Target Group Index surveys with more specific questions on film audiences.

The main arguments were as follows:

- Child audiences are important at certain times of the year and for certain films – the survey needed to start younger.
- On television the audiences (both size and composition) are measured for every minute of the day throughout the year (see Chapter 3). Cinema cannot get away with a bland statement that the audiences are always much the same.
- For distributors film research is product research. Most is historical, and it is often published too late to influence the current release of a film. However, when a new film is to be launched it is useful for a distributor to have evidence from comparable past films when deciding to whom the new release will appeal.
- The cinema contractors often sell advertising packages in which the advertisements follow the film (or films). The audiences for such packages need to be predicted, and again evidence from the past is required.
- The cinema advertising industry operates a voluntary system whereby advertisements for alcoholic drinks are withdrawn from a performance where the feature film is such that 25 per cent or more of the audience is likely to be under 18 years old. Evidence from past films is needed to support this system.

The main CAVIAR survey is carried out in October–November each year with a quota sample of about 3,100 covering all age groups over 5 years old. The interviews are conducted face-to-face by Carrick James Market Research (and from 1992 by BMRB International).

As far as cinema is concerned the main questions cover:

• Frequency and recency of cinema-going (similar to the NRS questions).

• Detailed record of visits in the last two months including the cinemas attended and the films seen. The certificate of the film is recorded and the films are also classified by type according to a 52–point index.

• Attendance at any of a list of 60 films during the previous year. This list includes 48 main releases and 12 'art' films.

• Other questions include the source of information about the film, who goes with whom, means of transport, and interest in other facilities at the cinema site. A question was recently asked on reasons for going to multiplex cinemas.

An additional survey known as the CAVIAR Film Monitor is carried out every other month with a sample of about 4,000 people aged over 7 with a question on attendance at 24 current release films. The film profile data are so important that it is not always possible to wait for the annual survey for the data. Also the Monitor produces information on many more films.

Table 7.5 illustrates some of the CAVIAR 9 data. Clearly there are large differences by age group. Thus 30 per cent of the audience of *The Little Mermaid* is under 12. For *The Naked Gun* 66 per cent are between 12 and 24. *Dances with Wolves* is exceptional in having 45 per cent of its audience aged over 35. Table 7.6 shows the top 10 films of the last decade.

CAMPAIGN EVALUATION

There are different media options available to advertisers using cinema. The most popular and cost-effective route is the Audience Discount Package (ADP), accounting for about 70 per cent of air-time sold. To qualify for the ADP, advertisers must use all screens within an entire ISBA Region (or group of regions). The ADP, representing a significant discount on other buying routes, is costed on an audience basis using a fixed cost per thousand over the campaign period. The admissions potential of the campaign and therefore cost for the areas used are agreed on the basis of the latest Gallup audience data. Once booked, the screen time is non pre-emptible.

Advertisers using the ADP are given feedback on weekly admissions to their campaigns using data from the Gallup Admission Monitor. A typical example is shown in Table 7.7.

Projected reach and frequency on ADP campaigns are estimated from

Table 7.5 The CAA CAVIAR 9 Survey: cinema profiles, 1991

	Total (000's)	5–6 (%)	7–11 (%)	12–17 (%)	18–24 (%)	25–34 (%)	35+ (%)	Male (%)	Female (%)	ABC1 (%)	C2DE (%)
Population	52,119	2	7	7	12	17	55	49	51	42	58
Selected mainstream releases:											
The Little Mermaid (U)	2,225	6	24	15	11	25	19	40	60	57	43
Cyrano de Bergerac (U)	450	–	–	9	26	38	27	59	41	70	30
Home Alone (PG)	5,099	1	13	23	29	15	19	49	51	51	49
Robin Hood: Prince of Thieves (PG)	6,026	1	13	19	23	18	26	53	47	58	42
Dances with Wolves (12)	2,798	–	–	14	17	24	45	47	53	60	40
Naked Gun 2½: The Smell of Fear (12)	2,434	–	–	31	35	21	13	57	43	54	46
Sleeping with the Enemy (15)	2,390	–	–	13	39	26	22	39	61	55	45
Terminator 2: Judgment Day (15)	4,536	–	–	17	36	31	16	60	40	52	48
The Silence of the Lambs (18)	4,453	–	–	–	37	31	32	53	47	59	41
Selected art film summary	986	–	–	7	25	39	29	54	46	65	35

Visits by certificate August–October 1991	% of visits	7–11 (%)	12–17 (%)	18–24 (%)	25–34 (%)	35+ (%)	Male (%)	Female (%)	ABC1 (%)	C2DE (%)
U	8	24	8	5	30	33	43	57	57	43
PG	33	16	22	21	17	24	51	49	55	45
12	14	–	25	16	23	36	46	54	60	40
15	32	–	15	38	27	20	59	41	52	48
18	13	–	–	42	40	18	55	45	52	48
All visits	100	7	17	27	25	24	53	47	55	45
Multiplex visits	52	7	15	34	24	20	53	47	54	46

Table 7.6   The top 10 films of the last decade

Film title	Audience 7 years+ (millions)
ET (1983)	11.3
Ghostbusters (1985)	8.5
Crocodile Dundee 2 (1988)	7.7
Who Framed Roger Rabbit? (1989)	7.2
Crocodile Dundee (1988)	7.0
Jungle Book (1984)	6.4
Ghost (1990)	6.3
Return of the Jedi (1983)	6.3
Indiana Jones and the Last Crusade (1989)	6.3
Robin Hood: Prince of Thieves (1991)	6.0

Source: CAVIAR

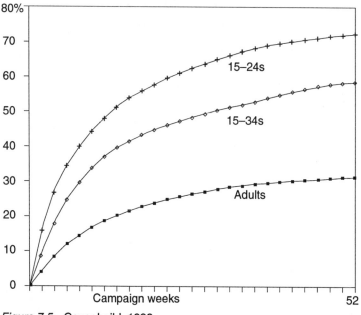

Figure 7.5   Cover build, 1992
Source: NRS, 1991

analysis of NRS, TGI and CAVIAR data using the probability model described earlier. The Cinema Advertising Association produce extensive cover and frequency guides annually which can be used to evaluate potential reach against demographic groups by ISBA Area (NRS, 1991;

Table 7.7   Cinema admissions estimate

Client	Brand X
Total admissions contracted	8,590,065
Commercial length	30 seconds
Campaign period	06/09/91–05/12/91
No weeks	7
Agency	Agency Y
Statement date	13/01/92

Advertising week commencing*	Total UK admissions	Total RSA admissions**	No. of RSA screens used	Total RSA campaign admissions
01/11/91	1,431,116	1,215,645	752	715,869
08/11/91	1,379,152	1,188,973	0	0
15/11/91	1,262,092	1,076,335	838	677,789
22/11/91	1,281,491	1,092,253	0	0
29/11/91	1,150,180	980,866	743	502,486

Total RSA campaign admissions to date: 9,019,568

Campaign performance to date

Actual admissions delivered	9,019,568
Targated admissions for period	8,590,065
% difference	+5.0% final***

Notes: * Cinema advertising is sold in units of one week
** There are two advertising contractors in the UK, the example here is of an RSA advertising campaign
***In this particular example the campaign over-delivered on admissions by 5%

CAVIAR, 1990). Network cover build (using all screens) is illustrated in Figure 7.5.

Analysis of TGI data enables campaign cover and frequency to be estimated against users of brands and product groups as opposed to standard demographics. For example, campaign achievement against purchasers of Levi jeans or frequent purchasers of compact discs can be analysed.

Using the coverage and frequency model, evaluation of mixed schedule campaigns is also possible. The effect of introducing cinema to a press or television campaign can be analysed.

Cinema-goers are, almost by definition, less likely to be heavy viewers of television, as shown in Figure 7.6. By including cinema in a mixed media campaign, we usually increase the number of people who see the

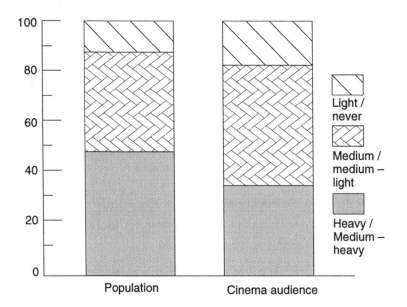

Figure 7.6   Viewing of ITV
Source: NRS, 1991

campaign at least once at the expense of repeated impacts among those
who may see it more often than is necessary.

Other buying routes used for cinema air-time include film packages.
These are available by title or by type of film, for example, Disney or Art
film packages. CAVIAR data, in particular the bi-monthly film Monitor,
are used to provide campaign feedback on the audience demographic
structure.

QUALITATIVE MEASUREMENTS

During the last 40 years the CAA has carried out numerous studies to
measure the recall, communicative power and popularity of particular
cinema commercials. The results looked good, but did not answer directly
the key question, 'How does the impact of cinema advertising compare
with that of television?'

To answer this question the CAA sought to measure the impact of the
same advertisement on both cinema and television after one exposure. For

example, in 1985 it conducted a survey for Insignia (Marplan, 1985), which is a range of men's toiletries. At that time it had a new commercial for a new product. The commercial was screened on London Weekend Television on the same evening that it was shown on cinema screens in the London area – for the first time on both media.

The research was carried out by Marplan, which recruited a sample of 20–34 year olds at the cinema and re-interviewed them the next day by telephone. The television sample was secured the next day as far as possible from the Marplan television panel, but they qualified only if they had seen the programme in which the advertisement appeared. The results are shown in Table 7.8.

Table 7.8   The Insignia survey

	Cinema	Television
Sample	200	97
Seeing advertisements	85%	68%
Recalling Insignia:		
Spontaneous	7%	1%
Product-group prompted	20%	3%
Brand-prompted	47%	11%
Total recall	74%	15%

Source: CAA/Marplan 1985

The spontaneous recall is without any prompt. The product-group-prompted recall is achieved by asking the question again after reference has been made to male toiletries. The brand-prompted recall is recorded after the respondents have been given a list of four product names that they might have seen.

This research (which has also been carried out with other products) demonstrates that cinema advertising can achieve a level of recall after one exposure which can only be achieved on television after numerous exposures (Gallup, 1990b). The same study also investigates with further questions the power of the commercial to communicate and the appreciation of the advertisement by the public. Unfortunately, the fragmentation of television audiences with more channels is making it more difficult to repeat this research. If the rating for the programme is low, the recruitment of a panel who have seen it is correspondingly expensive.

FILM TRACKING

A film distributor can obtain preliminary evidence (in CAVIAR or similar surveys) from the audience to comparable past films when deciding to whom a new film will appeal. These predictions sometimes prove to be inaccurate. As the launch of a new release gets under way more direct evidence of success related to the actual film concerned is needed. For film distributors the answer lies in film tracking; this is carried out weekly with a minimum sample of 400 cinema-goers plus samples of special interest cinema-goers by the National Research Group. The survey plots prompted awareness and desire to see over time. Other questions relate to choice among competition, source of information, remembered film elements from the advertising, and so on. In this way the film distributor can see the extent to which the launch publicity is succeeding.

ANALYSIS OF DRIVE TIME

In developing new cinemas the exhibitors look carefully at the population, its size and profile, the presence of competitors, the attributes of the site and particularly its ease of access for potential cinema-goers in the market area. We know from the CAVIAR 9 Survey that 77 per cent of patrons to multiplex cinemas arrive at the cinema by car.

Most cinema exhibitors would subscribe to one of the several geodemographic agencies to derive population numbers and profiles within nominated drive times around the site. Frequently, 10, 15 and 20 minutes drive time bands would be used, with 30 minutes in rural areas. As a rule of thumb most operators would be looking for about a quarter of a million people resident within 20 minutes of the site to justify the investment in a new multiplex. Such a rule takes no account of competition, which must always be considered. Operators will also pay particular heed to the numbers of 15 to 24-year-olds within the catchment area who (as we have seen) make up the core market of frequent cinema-goers.

EUROPEAN CINEMA

In most other European countries information on cinema admissions and screens is compiled from government sources, with information used for taxation purposes. The most recent data available is for 1990; admissions and screens for selected countries are shown in Table 7.9. The admissions in some European countries have slipped badly over the last ten years.

Table 7.9   International cinema, 1990

	Cinema screens	Admission (millions)	Admissions per capita
Belgium	382	16.2	1.6
Denmark	357	9.6	1.9
France	4,518	121.8	2.2
W. Germany	3,222	102.5	1.7
Greece	600	16.5	1.6
Ireland	171	7.4	2.1
Italy	3,249	90.5	1.6
Luxembourg	17	0.5	1.3
Netherlands	426	14.6	1.0
Portugal	250	11.0	1.0
Spain	1,733	78.5	2.0
UK	1,685	97.2	1.7
EC (12)	16,650	566.3	1.7
USA	23,689	1,056.6	4.2
East Europe	13,181	3,953.7	9.3

Source: *Screen Digest*/national agencies

However, the exhibitors may find encouragement in the experience of the UK where a low point was reached in 1984 followed by a substantial recovery.

FUTURE DEVELOPMENTS

As media fragment and competition between them increases, there will be an unprecedented need for different media to justify their inclusion on campaign schedules. For media that are in many ways comparable, e.g. competing satellite or television channels, discrimination of audiences and how channels are viewed – for leisure, information, and so on – will become important. Cinema is not directly comparable with other media; the impact is unparalleled, as shown in the Insignia research, and is viewed in a very different way from other media, accompanied by a sense of occasion as opposed to a habitual viewing.

Future research will need to address the real value that cinema can bring to multi-media campaigns. Measurement of the contribution of different media to specific client advertising objectives is needed as opposed to mere feedback on audiences likely to be exposed to commercials.

REFERENCES

CAVIAR (1990) *Coverage and Frequency Guide: School Holiday Weeks*, London, Cinema Advertising Association.

CAVIAR (1991a) Tables and Commentary volumes, London, Cinema Advertising Association.

CAVIAR (1991b) Brochure, London, Cinema Advertising Association.

CAVIAR (1991c) *Datacard*, London, Cinema Advertising Association.

CAVIAR 9 Survey (1991) London, Cinema Advertising Association.

Gallup (1990a) *A Proposal for Operating a Continuous Monitor of Cinema Admissions, July, London, Cinema Advertising Association.*

Gallup (1990b) *Advertising Impact Study: Terry's Le Box Chocolates*, London, Cinema Advertising Association.

Institute of Travel and Tourism (1991) 'Effective Multi-client Research – Example from Cinema and Video Industry', paper to ITT/AEMRI Seminar, November, London.

Kent, R. A. (1993) *Marketing Research in Action*, London, Routledge.

Marplan (1985) *A Report on the Impact of Cinema Advertising: Insignia Men's Toiletries*, London, Cinema Advertising Association.

National Readership Survey (1991) *Coverage and Frequency Guide, Jan.–Dec.*, London, Cinema Advertising Association.

Chapter 8

Measuring media audiences
The way ahead

Raymond Kent

From the chapters that constitute this book, it is possible to discern a number of trends and developments that are common to all the media and which give some clue or feeling as to how things are likely to develop in the next few years. It is the purpose of this concluding chapter to draw together some of these pointers to the way ahead.

In the UK the average person spends about 3.8 hours a day viewing television, about 3 hours listening to the radio, and about 20 minutes reading a newspaper or magazine – some 7 hours per day in all. This is a high proportion of the time any person spends at home and awake on any day, even bearing in mind that it is not necessarily the same people watching television and listening to the radio or reading the output of the print media. In fact, the relationship between the use of the media is one issue that has not been tackled by any of the contributors to this volume. Are those people who watch a lot of television also those people who listen a lot or listen little to the radio? Are heavy readers also heavy or light radio listeners? This is one area that requires a lot of further analysis, particularly with the development of multi-media advertising campaigns.

It is also clear that these patterns of media use vary considerably from country to country. According to Kasari (1993) the Irish listen to radio or watch television for a total of 7.6 hours per day, 50 per cent of which is radio. The UK, Poland and Italy have the lowest share of radio (about 30 per cent), while Denmark, Flemish Belgium and Finland have very high radio shares (about 60 per cent). Patterns are clearly very complex.

It is necessary to bear in mind that differences between countries at least in part may be a result of differences in research organisation, methodology and technique. The contributions in this volume make it clear that different procedures produce different results. Thus radio diaries tend to produce more listening to radio than recall in face-to-face interviews; yet Ireland and Czechoslovakia, with some of the highest reported radio listening in the world, both use the latter technique (Kasari, 1993). When contracts for media audience research are renegotiated, the specification often changes – usually, and quite reasonably, to take account of changing media contexts. However, this can make year-on-year comparisons somewhat clouded. Thus adding in estimates of video playback into consolidated television ratings in the UK made the 1991 audiences look bigger than for 1990 (although this did not, of course, affect audience share).

Making any kind of comparison is thus fraught with difficulty. Some of these difficulties will be exacerbated and some will be alleviated by trends and developments in media audience measurement generally. The main trends that can be identified from the foregoing chapters include:

- the growing fragmentation of audiences,
- increased media choice for audiences, whether it is more television channels or videos to watch, more radio stations to listen to, more newspapers, magazines or books to read, or more cinema films to go to,
- intensifying media industry competition, giving advertisers more choice,
- moves towards the harmonisation of research methodology through the setting up of bodies like the European Broadcasting Union or the European Association of Advertising Agencies, the establishment of joint industry committees, or the elimination of competing systems,
- the development of pan-European and multi-country advertising,
- increased involvement of the subscribers and users of media audience data in the specification and design of the research,
- deregulation and privatisation of the media.

While harmonisation will, clearly, facilitate comparisons, the other trends are likely to make them infinitely more difficult. Thus audiences are fragmenting geographically, ethnically, socially, economically and politically. A hint of the difficulties this raises for media audience measurement is given by Kasari (1993), who suggests that for some countries like Belgium and Switzerland, the use of the media varies considerably by language group. Thus the Flemish-speaking Belgian spends 3.7 hours a day with radio on an average day, but the French-speaking Belgian only 1.9 hours. A German-speaking Swiss listens for about 2.8 hours a day; a French-Swiss only 1.9 hours.

Some developments are specific to the particular medium. Thus for television the development of cable and satellite television, video cassette recorders, camcorders, computers, compact discs and so on, will all impact on the ways in which television is used, and on the ways in which the various pieces of equipment can be linked together. New technologies may be required to identify what is actually happening on the screen, and it may become necessary to meter individual viewing, for example with the use of 'passive' sensing and image recognition equipment. The problem here, besides the cost and acceptability both to viewers and to media owners, is that piecemeal development and use of such equipment will result, once more, in deharmonisation of research methodologies. It is more likely that, in the foreseeable future, the use of the peoplemeter will become universal and that improvements in accuracy will be achieved more economically by increasing sample sizes.

At the same time the trend towards shorter advertisements on television mentioned by Sharot, added to the growing concerns about the number of people who use VCRs and remote controls to 'zip' and 'zap' the ads, will put increased pressure to develop ever more refined peoplemeter equipment. While some doubts have been raised about the validity of television ratings, particularly for commercials, there is a trend towards seeing ratings as only part of what any measurement system should be addressing. Audience appreciation of programmes and advertisements will probably become a vital part of the analysis along with diagnostic information to help explain the crude scores. In the UK the Broadcasters Audience Research Board (BARB) is currently investigating options for a new method of measuring audience appreciation. A key consideration is whether there should be a separate panel, a regular survey, or whether it should use the existing peoplemeter panel.

Unlike television, with its peoplemeters and its joint industry committees, there is little common ground in the way Europeans measure their radio audiences. Some use diaries, some use recall with either face-to-face or telephone interviewing. As Twyman points out, the increasing numbers of radio stations and the growing variety of reception modes will increase the problems for both recall and diaries. These techniques may need to be combined to improve accuracy, or some new technology such as the wristwatch meter that recognises radio signals will need to be developed.

In readership research it is the development of computer-assisted telephone interviewing (CATI) and computer-assisted personal interviewing (CAPI) that has, and will probably continue, to have the greatest impact. With the development of computer screens and lap-top, even hand-held, computers, there may be no reason why not only the questions and the answers can be stored electronically, but prompt materials such as newspaper mastheads could also be displayed. Videotext and teletext technologies may be used for presenting a readership questionnaire. The barcodes on printed materials could be used by a panel of readers to record what, when and how they are reading. Metering systems are perhaps further into the future with microchip insertions into the pages of printed materials to sense the flexing of pages that occurs when a publication is read. Once a dominant medium, outdoor posters have been something of an advertising backwater, taking only 4 per cent of national adspend in the UK. However, according to Santini (1993) fresh life is reawakening in the UK and elsewhere in Europe with the rediscovery of the medium's unique qualities. The industry's attempts to revive itself have been both gallant and persistent. Poster sites have been refurbished, information from OSCAR is used to provide advertisers with computerised maps of networks of panels along with data on the size and structure of audiences delivered by each site. New technology may result in posters with liquid-crystal display screens; there will probably be fewer but better sites that are integrated and planned into the urban environment. Geographic information systems have enormous potential for the development of cost-effective poster campaigns. Better site-audience estimates could be achieved if traffic data from the Department of Transport could be integrated into the system. In-car navigation systems hold out the prospect of extremely accurate tracking of routes taken by drivers. Pedestrian flow figures from shopping centres and audiences to transport media could be integrated into the system. Hypothetical campaigns could be modelled and simulated with different weights and types of campaign.

The contribution by Chilton and Butler brings out another feature of media audience measurement that will become increasingly important: as media fragment, as competition between them intensifies, and with growing emphasis on multi-media campaigns, so each medium will need to justify its inclusion in any schedule. However, feedback on the sizes and composition of audiences exposed to the advertisements will no longer be adequate; it will also be necessary to look at the impact and contribution each medium can make to client advertising objectives, whether this be brand awareness, loyalty, company image, perceived value, and so on. Future research will need to address the real value that cinema can bring to multi-media campaigns, taking into account that it is viewed in a very different way to other media.

REFERENCES

Kasari, H. J. (1993) 'European Radio Audiences: Differences, and the Need for Harmonised Research Methodologies', *Admap*, February.
Santini, P. E. (1993) 'An Old Giant Stirs: Once a Dominant Medium, Fresh Life is Reawakening the UK Poster Industry', *Admap*, April.

Index